The
Book *of*
Christmas

hardie grant books

by Christopher Winn

The Hidden Stories Behind our Festive Traditions

Contents

Introduction

I'm dreaming of a white Christmas …
Chestnuts roasting on an open fire …
Mistletoe and wine … A partridge in a pear
tree … Mary's boy child … Yule-tide carols
being sung by a choir … Deck the halls with
boughs of holly … Santa Claus is comin'
to town … Jingle bells, jingle bells, jingle
all the way … I wish it could be Christmas
every day …

Christmas. The biggest party in the
world. The most widely celebrated
festival on Earth – it is estimated that
well over half of the world's population
actively participates in Christmas.

Why?

That is a good question and one that deserves an answer.

Well, there isn't an answer, at least not a definitive one. There are in fact many answers, all of them with a contribution to make to the truth about Christmas. Over the years great scholars and gifted academics have wrestled each other to a bloodied standstill over the question of Christmas, only to retire baffled and broken. Even I, once described by a perceptive newspaper columnist as the 'greatest living authority' on something or other, even I must concede I don't fully have the answer to Christmas. But together, dear Reader, we might be able to come up with a pretty good idea of what Christmas is all about, and so here, for your delectation, is what I have discovered. Hopefully, by the time you have reached the end of the book, you will have enough information to make up your own mind. You will certainly have learned some interesting stuff. I have.

O Come all ye Faithful …

A Christmas Timetable

BC	Midwinter festivals of the Druids, Norse Yule and Roman Saturnalia
AD	
1	Jesus Christ born in Bethlehem
129	The first carol, 'Gloria in Excelsis Deo' ('The Angel's Hymn') is sung in Rome
274	Winter Solstice, 25 December: Temple in Rome dedicated to *Sol Invictus*, the Unconquered Sun
313	Edict of Milan legitimises Christianity throughout the Roman Empire under Emperor Constantine I
325	Council of Nicaea, convened by Emperor Constantine and attended by St Nicholas of Myra, affirms that Jesus Christ is the Son of God
336	First known Christmas as recorded in the Chronography of 354
337	Emperor Constantine becomes the first Christian Emperor when he is baptised on his deathbed
380	Emperor Theodosius I declares Christianity to be the official religion of the Roman Empire

432	First midnight mass, Basilica of St Mary Maggiore, Rome
440	Church authorities fix the date of Christ's birth as 25 December
567	Council of Tours proclaims the 12 days from Christmas to Epiphany as a sacred and festive season
597	First Christmas Day in England. St Augustine baptises over 10,000 English converts at Canterbury
935	Murder of Good King Wenceslas in Prague, Czech Republic
1025	First documented crib, St Maria del Presepe, Naples
1066	Christmas Day: William the Conqueror crowned in Westminster Abbey
1223	First Nativity play staged by St Francis of Assisi in Greccio, Italy, against the backdrop of the first live crib
1296	First recorded winter market, Vienna's *Dezembermarkt,* Austria
1419	First reported Christmas tree, Freiburg, Germany

1434	First Christmas market held in Dresden, Germany
1492	Christmas Eve: one of Christopher Columbus' ships, the *Santa Maria*, runs aground on the island of Hispanola, modern-day Haiti. Columbus uses the wreck of the ship to build a fortress on the island and leaves the crew behind to man it. He christens the settlement, the first European colony established in the New World, Puerto de la Navidad, meaning Port Christmas
1510	First recorded Christmas tree put up in Riga, Latvia
1595	First glass Christmas ornaments produced in Lauscha, Germany
1610	Tinsel invented in Nuremberg, Germany
1777	Christmas Eve: Captain Cook discovers a small island in the Indian Ocean 220 miles (350 km) south of Java. He names it Christmas Island
1800	First Christmas tree in Britain, at Queen's Lodge, Windsor
1843	Henry Cole invents the Christmas card
1848	Silver-lined glass baubles invented, Lauscha, Germany
1882	First electric Christmas tree lights, New York, USA

1891   First personalised Christmas card sent
             by Annie Oakley from Scotland to her
             family in America

1898   First stamp marked Christmas
             issued, Canada

1914   Christmas Day Truce. British and
             German soldiers meet in no man's land
             on the Western Front in France and
             Belgium to exchange gifts and play
             impromptu games of football

1922   Christmas Eve: BBC broadcast the first
             play ever written especially for radio, a
             Christmas play for children by Phillis Twig
             called *The Truth about Father Christmas*

1953   First set of official Christmas stamps issued
             by the Australian Post Office

1965   First Christmas song broadcast from space.
             Sung by the astronauts on Gemini VI
             accompanied by a harmonica and sleigh
             bells during a spoof report of seeing Santa
             Claus go past in his sleigh

1968   First Christmas greeting sent from space:
             'Good luck, a Merry Christmas, and God bless
             all of you – all of you on the good Earth.' Sent
             by Apollo 8 astronaut Frank Borman while in
             orbit around the Moon

2001   25 December: first Christmas Day
             of the third millennium

In the introduction we posed the question, 'Why is Christmas the most widely celebrated festival on Earth?' In other words, what is it about Christmas that appeals to so many people, no matter what their religion or nationality?

To answer that, we need to find out what Christmas is and where it comes from.

Let's begin with what Christmas actually is.

Christmas is exactly what it says it is, 'Christ's Mass', or the mass that is observed on Christ's birthday.

Mass comes from the Latin *missa*, meaning to dismiss or send forth. In the same way that a 'missionary' is someone who is sent forth to spread the Word of God, so at the end of mass, Christian worshippers are sent forth to live a Christian life.

The name Christ comes from the Greek *Xristos* (pronounced Khristos), a translation of the Hebrew word *Masiah* or Messiah, meaning 'anointed one'. The often used abbreviation Xmas is derived from the first letter 'X' in *Xristos*.

So Christmas is the time we are sent forth into the world to proclaim the birth of the Messiah.

So what is the story behind the birth that we celebrate and go forth in the world to proclaim?

The story behind the birth of Christ is known as the Nativity, from the Latin *natal*, meaning birth, and is told in the Bible, in the Gospel of St Luke. The following page, in very simplified form, details the plot.

The Nativity

A little over 2,000 years ago, the angel Gabriel appeared to a young virgin by the name of Mary, who lived in Nazareth in Galilee and was engaged to be married to a carpenter called Joseph. Gabriel announced to Mary that she would bear a child who would be the son of God and should be called Jesus. Joseph was visited by another angel who told him that it was the will of God that he should marry Mary and bring up the child as his son. Not long before Jesus was due to be born, a decree went out from the Roman Emperor Caesar Augustus that there should be a census of all those who lived in the Roman Empire, and that everyone should register in the town where their family came from. Joseph was of the House of David and his ancestors came from Bethlehem, some 70 miles (112 km) away.

So Joseph and Mary, who was by now his wife, set off on the long journey south. When they arrived in Bethlehem there was no room at the inn because so many people had come to register, and so Joseph and Mary had to take shelter in a stable with the animals, the ox and the ass. And there Mary gave birth to her first-born son, Jesus, and she wrapped him in swaddling clothes and laid him in a manger of straw. That night an angel of the Lord appeared to some shepherds in the field who were watching over their flock, and told them of the birth in the city of David of a Saviour, Christ the Lord. And the shepherds hurried to Bethlehem and found Jesus in the stable, lying in a manger just as the angel had said, and they bowed down and worshipped him as the Messiah.

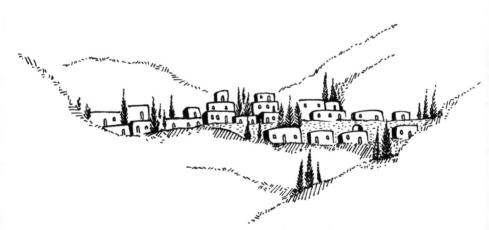

But why do people who are not Christian celebrate the Christian festival of Christmas?

Because Christmas absorbed, adapted and eventually replaced many of the pre-Christian and pagan festivals that were celebrated by different peoples and civilisations around the world. At the same time, Christmas retained essential elements of those festivals and clothed them in Christianity. Through the centuries, secular features have been added to the religious aspects of Christmas, features such as shopping and feasting that can be enjoyed by everyone, regardless of their faith or nationality. Christmas, in fact, has come to mean whatever you want it to mean.

Let's explore the origins of Christmas a bit more.

Christmas has its earliest origins in the midwinter festivals that were observed by pagan societies who lived their lives by the rhythms of the seasons. Midwinter was the darkest time of year, and the ceremonies revolved around hopes and prayers for the return and rebirth of the Sun. The Druids believed that the Sun stood still for twelve days in midwinter and so they would burn a log during these twelve days to banish the darkness and protect them from evil spirits. This was similar to the twelve-day Norse festival of Yule during which people would sit around bonfires singing and feasting and drinking to while away the dark hours.

Yule, incidentally, is derived from 'Jul', one of the many names given to the Norse Sun god Odin. The word Jul comes from the old Germanic word *hweal*, meaning a wheel, which is how Norsemen thought of the Sun and its circular course through the heavens. Hence, when the Sun god Odin, or Jul, visited the Earth in his chariot for twelve days in December this was known as Yuletide, a word we now apply to Christmas.

The Romans had their own midwinter festival called Saturnalia, which shared many of the elements of Yule, as we shall see later.

In the 4th century, these midwinter festivals were appropriated and 'Christianised' when the Roman Emperor Constantine I legalised Christianity throughout the Empire. Later, in AD 380, the Emperor Theodosius declared that Christianity was to be the official religion of the Roman Empire. The first known Christmas Day was recorded in the Chronography of 354 as taking place in AD 336 with the words '25 Dec.: natus Christus in Betleem Judeae' (25 December, Christ born in Bethlehem, Judea).

Christianity and the celebration of Christmas were then spread east and west throughout the Roman Empire by decree and later, after the fall of the Western Roman Empire, by missionaries sent out from Rome by the Pope.

Christmas was brought to England, for example, in AD 597, with the arrival in Kent of St Augustine, who was sent by Pope Gregory the Great to convert the heathen Anglo-Saxons of Kent to Christianity. In that same year, to mark the first Christmas Day in England, St Augustine baptised over 10,000 English converts in a field outside St Martin's Church in Canterbury. The Venerable Bede writes in the 8th century that Christmas was, by then, well established in England as one of the three major festivals of the church year along with Easter and Epiphany.

By the end of the first millennium, most of the peoples of Europe had been converted to Christianity and when, in the 16th and 17th centuries, the European nations began to colonise new worlds, they took Christmas in all its various forms with them, to North America, to India, Malaysia, China and Africa, and to the southern hemisphere, South America and Australasia.

The Victorians, who in their time presided over a quarter of the world, reinvigorated Christmas, thanks in large part to Prince Albert and Charles Dickens, and then took it out across the British Empire to all four corners of the globe. But the Victorians were businessmen as well as missionaries and they promoted trade as well as Christmas. Many people around the world who were not interested in the religious aspects of Christmas could nevertheless see the commercial potential of Christmas and throughout the 20th century Christmas became less about religion and more about shopping and commerce. In many ways Christmas has now come full circle, from a feast for pagans to a feast for consumers.

Why 25 December?

Christmas celebrates the birth of Christ, not Christ's birthday. In other words 25 December is Christ's official birthday, not his real birthday. No one knows the date on which Jesus was actually born. The Bible doesn't tell us, although scholars have tried to extract clues from St Luke's story of the Nativity. For instance, on the day that Jesus was born, 'there were in the same country shepherds abiding in the field, keeping watch over their flock by night.'

Now shepherds would only have their sheep out in the fields during the summer months and would bring them home in the autumn. So it would seem that Jesus must have been born in late summer or early autumn, September, perhaps, or at the latest October. But no one knows for sure.

Early Christians would not have celebrated Jesus' real birthday anyway, even if they had known when it was. Birthdays weren't considered worthy of celebration – in fact there are only two direct mentions of birthdays in the whole Bible.

The day on which a saint died was considered much more significant, as this was the day when the saint became one with God. Hence, Easter, when Christ died on the Cross, was, and still is, the most important religious celebration for the Christian Church.

Now, when Christianity became the official religion of the Romans, the authorities decided they needed a festival to replace the rowdy pagan winter festivals of yore, which were a byword for drunkenness, lewd behaviour and over-indulgence. But rather than causing upset by punishing people or banning them from observing the revelries they had enjoyed since ancient times, the Church decided to entice people in by quietly absorbing those festivities into a Christian celebration instead.

But what to celebrate? Christ's death was already celebrated at Easter. So why not honour his birth instead? And that is what they did.

***
Odds and Ends

The fact that Christ has an official or ceremonial birthday
(25 December) is not so unusual. Many heads of state have
official birthdays. British kings and queens, for instance, have
an official birthday in June, regardless of when their actual
birthday falls. The present Queen, Elizabeth II, was born on
21 April but celebrates her official birthday with Trooping
the Colour on the second Saturday in June. This tradition
was started by King George II in 1748. His birthday was in
November, not a good time to have a birthday parade because
in Britain the weather can be pretty awful then. So he decided
that his birthday parade should be in the summer when there
was more likelihood of good weather.

***

The 25th of December was chosen as the official day of Christ's
birth for a number of reasons. By the calendar they were using
in those days, 25 December was the shortest day of the year,
the day when the Sun reached its lowest point and began to rise
again in the heavens. It was the climax of the Roman winter
festival of Saturnalia, the day known and celebrated by the
Romans as *Sol Invictus* or *dies solis invicti nati*, the birthday of the
Unconquerable Sun, and the Christian Church translated this
smoothly into the Birthday of the Everlasting Son.

Meanwhile 25 December fitted in rather well with another
Christian festival, the Feast of the Annunciation. The
Annunciation was the moment when the angel Gabriel appeared
to the Virgin Mary and told her that she would be visited by
the Holy Spirit, that she would conceive a son to be called
Jesus, and that he would be the Son of God. This occasion is
celebrated on 25 March which, again by the calendar they
were using in those days, was the date of the spring equinox.
Now the spring equinox, according to an ancient and rather
mysterious calculation, equates to the fourth day of Creation,
when God said, 'Let there be Light.' In the same way, Light was
brought into the world when Jesus, known to Christians as the
Light of the World, was conceived on 25 March. So, if Jesus
was conceived on 25 March, then nine months later would be
25 December. Simple, really.

Io Saturnalia!

The Roman festival of Saturnalia was held in honour of the agricultural deity Saturn, god of sowing (*satus* is the Latin for sowing), and marked the end of the autumn growing season. The festival was basically the Roman update of all the pagan winter festivals that had gone before, from the worship of the Persian sun god Mithras (whose birthday was 25 December) to the Celtic and Norse festivals of fire.

Saturnalia was the reward for the long, hard year of toil in the fields. The crops were gathered in, the autumn sowing was done, the cattle had been slaughtered and there was plenty of meat for feasting. All work and business ceased. Shops were closed. The days were short, so there was little you could do except party.

Since the reign of Saturn was thought to have been a Golden Age of peace and plenty when all were equal and there were no masters and servants, the rules were relaxed during Saturn's festival; social and moral norms were inverted, informal clothes were worn, and slaves were even allowed to misbehave and disrespect their masters. Indeed, roles were often reversed and masters waited on their slaves and servants. Drinking, overeating and roistering were the order of the day. People gave each other gifts. Described by the poet Catullus as 'the best of times', Saturnalia was a time of good will to all men, and just as we today bid people 'Merry Christmas', so Romans would go round hailing each other with the cry 'Io Saturnalia!'

Here is how Saturn himself describes his festival, in the words of the poet Lucian of Samosata, writing in the 2nd century AD.

'During my week the serious is barred; no business allowed. Drinking and being drunk, noise and games and dice, appointing of kings and feasting of slaves, singing naked, clapping of tremulous hands, an occasional ducking of corked faces in icy water – such are the functions over which I preside.'

Not so different from the average office Christmas party, if you think about it! And easy to see where the expression Saturnalian, meaning wild and debauched, comes from.

After Saturnalia and Sol Invictus came the festival of the Kalends, the first day of the month (hence calendar).

The Kalends of January were a time for everyone to rest and recover; houses were decorated with evergreens and candles to welcome in the New Year; and people were encouraged to give gifts to each other. They were especially encouraged to give gifts to the Emperor, such gifts being known as *votae*. As the 4th-century writer Libanius tells us,

'The impulse to spend seizes everyone. People are not only generous themselves, but also towards their fellow men. A stream of presents pours itself out on all sides. Another great quality of the festival is that it teaches men not to hold too fast to their money, but to part with it and let it pass into other hands.'

Clearly our modern Christmas has borrowed elements such as feasting and giving presents and lighting candles from Saturnalia and Kalends and other midwinter festivals. Christmas, it would appear, has pagan roots.

Let us now have a look at some of the customs and practices of Christmas to see if we can work out where they come from.

We begin with Advent.

Advent: The Tree

Christmas, in most people's minds, begins with Advent, but in fact, it doesn't.

The word Advent comes from the Latin *adventus*, meaning 'coming', and describes the period running up to Christmas during which Christians prepare for the coming of Christ on Christmas Day.

Advent is the first season of the Church year. The fourth Sunday before Christmas and the day on which Advent officially begins, is the first event in the Christian calendar. Advent was chosen to begin the Christian year because it represents the dark and uncertain time before Christ arrives in the world to spread the light.

Advent is not, however, the start of Christmas itself – that begins at sunset on Christmas Eve and lasts for twelve days until Epiphany on 6 January.

There are two aspects to the Coming of Christ for which we prepare in Advent. The First Coming is what we celebrate on Christmas Day, Christ's birth into the world in Bethlehem two thousand years ago. The Second Coming refers to Christ's Coming at the end of days to judge the living and the dead. The first two weeks of Advent focus on the Second Coming, and the hymns, prayers and readings in churches during this time are more solemn and reflective as they are designed to encourage thoughts of repentance before the last days. The second two weeks are more cheerful as we contemplate the impending birth of Christ and the joyous festivities that mark that happy occasion. The transition between contemplation and merriment occurs on the third Sunday in Advent and this is known as Gaudete Sunday, or the Sunday of Joy, from the Latin *gaudete* meaning 'rejoice'.

There are numerous different activities we associate with Advent, but one thing almost everybody does at some point in the run-up to Christmas is put up the Christmas tree.

The Christmas Tree

The Christmas tree stands at the very heart of Christmas. Originally it wasn't put up until Christmas Eve but nowadays, as the preparations for Christmas begin earlier and earlier, Christmas trees start to appear any time from 1 December onwards, or sometimes even before that.

Pope John Paul II called the Christmas tree a symbol of Christ, reminding Christians of the Tree of Life from Genesis, its evergreen nature a sign of everlasting life; but, like Christmas itself, the Christmas tree has its origins in pagan customs of long ago too. Since time immemorial, evergreen plants have been regarded as a symbol of hope and celebration, their greenery showing that life continues even in the bleak winter months. The ancient Egyptians adorned their homes with palm leaves and green rushes to celebrate the shortest day of the year, the winter solstice, when the Sun god Ra would begin to regain his strength and power. The Druids brought the branches of evergreen trees into their temples to signify resurgent life, and hung small gifts of nuts and fruit on the branches of pine trees as a gift for the winter deities. The Romans decorated their homes with greenery during the mid winter festival of Saturnalia.

There are many suggestions of how Christmas came by its tree. One of the more plausible is that the Christmas tree grew out of the Paradise Tree.

The Paradise Tree

Trees have always played an important role in Biblical stories. In the tale of Adam and Eve, for instance, a serpent hidden among the leaves of the Tree of Knowledge seduces Eve into eating the forbidden fruit from the Tree, and she in turn feeds it to Adam, with the result that they are banished from Paradise. In medieval times the story of Adam and Eve was told through plays called Paradise Plays that were performed throughout northern Europe for those who couldn't read. Centre stage in the Paradise Play was a representation of the Tree of Knowledge, known as the Paradise Tree, which was usually a large pine hung with red apples. Incidentally, it is the green of the evergreen and the red of the apples that gives us the traditional Christmas colours of red and green.

Paradise Plays fell from favour after the Protestant Reformation in the 16th century, but Paradise Trees were still put up in public places in many Northern European towns to mark the feast day of Adam and Eve, 24 December, and some German Catholic households would put up a wooden pyramid representing a Paradise Tree, in their homes on Christmas Eve.

St Boniface

Another suggestion gives credit for the Christmas tree to an Anglo-Saxon monk called Boniface, who was sent to Germany from England to convert the Germanic people to Christianity in the 8th century. The Saxons of northern Germany worshipped trees, in particular the oak tree, and often made human sacrifices to them by slaughtering someone at the base of the tree. One Christmas Eve, Boniface came across a pagan village where the villagers were preparing to mark the winter solstice by making the sacrifice of a young boy to Thor, the god of thunder, and the child was already laid out at the base of a sacred oak tree known as the Thunder Oak. Fortunately Boniface arrived just in time to prevent the tragedy. Using his staff he deflected the fatal blow aimed at the child and then took an axe to the oak tree and chopped it down, while the villagers stood back aghast and waited for Thor to strike Boniface down with his hammer. But of hammer blows came there none, and no thunderbolts either. Boniface just stood there, puffing a bit from his exertions, but otherwise entirely unscathed.

There are many accounts of what he went on to say to the villagers next, but the gist of it was along these lines:

'You see this small fir tree growing among the roots of the fallen oak? Make this your holy tree tonight. It is the tree of the Christ child for it points upwards to Heaven and its leaves are ever green, a sign of everlasting life. Take it into your own homes and let it shelter gifts of kindness and not deeds of blood.'

And, from that moment, people began to take a fir tree into their homes on Christmas Eve as a symbol of Jesus and good will to all mankind.

If this tale is correct, then while it may be true that the Christmas tree was introduced into Britain by a German queen, as we shall find out later, it was an English monk who gave the Germans the idea in the first place; an English monk with German ancestry, admittedly.

Martin Luther

The stories of the Paradise Tree and St Boniface both come from Catholic folklore. Protestants have their own theory, which is that it was Martin Luther, the Father of the Protestant Reformation in the early 16th century, who was the first person to take a Christmas tree indoors. And why did he do that?

Well, as he was walking through a snow-covered forest one Christmas Eve, Luther was struck by the beauty of the stars twinkling through the pine trees. He wanted his children to share the magic so he cut down a small tree, took it home and put lighted candles on the branches to replicate the stars and to honour Jesus Christ, the Light of the World. And then he placed the tree by the window so that passers-by could see it and rejoice with them.

The First Christmas Tree
(*Der Tannenbaum*)

There is no doubt that the idea of the Christmas tree came from Germany, where it is known as *der Tannenbaum*. The first Christmas tree which has been reliably chronicled was put up in 1419 in the town of Freiburg, in the Black Forest region of southwest Germany. It was decorated by the town bakers with fruits and nuts and, appropriately enough, baked goods, all of which were afterwards given to the children to eat on New Year's Day. Merchant guilds throughout northern Europe started to copy the idea and put up decorated trees outside their guild halls.

Another early example of a Christmas tree that we know about appeared in the Town Hall Square in Riga, the capital of Latvia, in 1510. A plaque set into the cobblestones outside the beautifully reconstructed 14th-century House of the Blackheads is engraved with the words 'The First New Year's Tree in Riga in 1510'. The Blackheads, by the way, were not pimples but a guild of unmarried German merchants whose name was taken from their patron saint St Maurice, who happened to be black. Apparently the Blackheads all wore black hats and danced around the tree, which was gaily decorated with paper roses symbolic of the Virgin Mary. Afterwards the tree was burned in a ceremony that neatly combined the rites of Christmas with the customs of the pagan festivals of the Druids and the Norsemen, where a Yule log, or even a whole tree, would be set alight and left to burn.

The First Christmas Tree in Britain

Contrary to what most people think, the first Christmas tree was not introduced into Britain by Prince Albert but by his grandmother-in-law (and distant cousin) Queen Charlotte, wife of George III. She put up Britain's first recorded Christmas tree in the drawing room of the Queen's Lodge in Windsor, in 1800.

Queen Charlotte came from the Grand Duchy of Mecklenburg-Strelitz in northern Germany, where it was the custom at Christmas-time to bring the branch of a yew tree into the house and dress it with candles. Charlotte had always enjoyed this, and when she came to England in 1761 to marry King George she was determined to carry on with the tradition. So every year she would install a yew branch in the drawing room at Windsor or Kew Palace, wherever the royal family was spending Christmas, and decorate it with candles and small presents such as sweets and toys and jewellery. The candles would be lit and everyone would gather round the branch to sing carols, after which Queen Charlotte herself would hand out the presents.

In 1800, Queen Charlotte decided to hold a big Christmas party at Windsor for the children of some of the prominent local families. There were so many people invited it soon became clear that one yew branch would never be able to hold enough presents for all the guests, and so Queen Charlotte had an entire tree installed in the middle of the room, which she dressed abundantly with candles and baubles and trinkets, sweets and toys.

Fortunately, Queen Charlotte's biographer, Dr John Watkins, has left us a vivid picture of this, Britain's first Christmas tree.

'In the middle of the room stood an immense tub with a yew tree placed in it, from the branches of which hung bunches of sweetmeats, almonds, and raisins in papers, fruits and toys, most tastefully arranged, and the whole illuminated by small wax candles. After the company had walked around and admired the tree, each child obtained a portion of the sweets which it bore together with a toy and then all returned home, quite delighted.'

Word of this wondrous tree spread quickly, and similar Christmas trees began to spring up in aristocratic houses all over England. Any evergreen tree would do, although pine and fir trees were favoured since they were a better shape, more plentiful, and with their soft and shallow roots tended to be easier to dig up.

Alas, it is no longer possible to see the room at Windsor where Queen Charlotte put up the first Christmas tree in Britain. Queen's Lodge, which stood close to the south curtain wall of Windsor Castle, was knocked down in 1823 on the orders of George IV because it spoiled his view of the Long Walk.

In 1840, Queen Charlotte's granddaughter, Queen Victoria, married Prince Albert, who was from the Bavarian town of Coburg, where the Christmas tree was already a well-established tradition much loved of Albert and his brother Ernst. Every year from then on, Prince Albert imported spruce trees from Coburg to use at Christmas so that his children could experience the 'delight in the Christmas trees' that he and Ernst had enjoyed as boys.

The Christmas tree became universally popular in Britain after a sketch of Prince Albert and Queen Victoria and their children, gathered around the Christmas tree at Windsor Castle, appeared on the front cover of the Christmas edition of the *Illustrated London News* in 1848. At first only relatively wealthy middle-class families could afford a tree, but Prince Albert did his bit by encouraging the putting up of Christmas trees in public spaces for the enjoyment of those who could not afford trees themselves, and also by sending ready decorated trees to the army barracks in Windsor and to local schools and hospitals.

As the appetite for Christmas trees grew, so the price became more affordable and thousands of trees were planted exclusively for use at Christmas. Today, some 8 million Christmas trees are sold in Britain every year.

Perhaps the most famous Christmas tree in Britain is the one put up in Trafalgar Square in London every year. Since 1947 the people of Oslo in Norway have donated a tall Norway spruce to the people of Britain as a thank you for Britain's support for Norway during the Second World War. The tree is cut in Norway in November in front of the British ambassador, along with the mayors of Oslo and Westminster, and then shipped by sea to be erected in Trafalgar Square at the beginning of December. It is decorated with hundreds of white lights which are switched on at a special ceremony on the first Thursday in December. For many in Britain this signals the start of Christmas, and throughout December people come from far and wide to sing carols around the tree. It is taken down on Twelfth Night and recycled for mulch.

Cracker Joke
Why are Christmas trees so bad at sewing?
—
They always drop their needles!

***
Odds and Ends

Although it was Queen Charlotte who put up what we think of as Britain's first official Christmas tree in 1800, it is possible that trees associated with Christmas existed in England long before that. Here is what the London historian John Stow wrote on the subject in his Survey of London, published in 1603:

'Against the feast of Christmas, euery mans house, as also their parish churches were decked with holme, Iuie, Bayes, and what does the season of the year afforded to be greene: The Conduits and Standards in the streetes were likewise garnished, amongst the which I reade in the yeare 1444, that by tempest of thunder and lightning, on the first of Februarie at night, Powles steeple was fiered, but with great labour quenched, and towarde the morning of Candlemas day, at the Leaden Hall in Cornhill, a Standarde of tree being set vp in midst of the pauement fast in the ground, nayled ful of Holme and Iuie, for disport of Christmas to the people, was torne vp, and cast downe by the malignant spirit.'

The oldest known Christmas tree alive in Britain today, a 100-foot- (30-metre-) high giant redwood tree, can be found growing in the gardens of Wrest Park in Bedfordshire.

It was planted by the then owner of the estate, Thomas de Grey, 2nd Earl de Grey, in 1856, at a time when the Christmas tree was becoming fashionable thanks to the royal family. Every year de Grey would have the tree uprooted and taken inside the house where it was decorated with sweets, candles and homemade baubles. Once the festivities were over, the tree was replanted in the garden until the following Christmas. Eventually it grew too big to be taken indoors and was left in peace until, in 2014, English Heritage, who now look after the estate, found an article about it in an old edition of *Gardener's Chronicle* from 1900. To celebrate Christmas in 2014, they placed a huge star on top of the tree and asked visitors to bedeck the lower branches with ribbons so that once again, after more than a century, the venerable old redwood resumed its role as a very special Christmas tree.

***

Christmas Trees around the World

Christmas trees can now be seen all over the world and some 300 million trees are grown every year to satisfy the demand. The Christmas tree has come a long way from Paradise...

USA

The Christmas tree was introduced into America in the 18th century by German immigrants to Pennsylvania and the Midwest. The idea of having a decorated Christmas tree inside the home, however, only really took off in America after the picture we mentioned previously, of the British royal family gathered around the Christmas tree at Windsor Castle, was printed in the popular American women's magazine *Godey's Lady Book* in 1850. This was the first picture of a decorated Christmas tree to be widely seen in America and the sketch, which had originally appeared on the cover of the *Illustrated London News* a couple of years earlier in 1848, was subtly altered to make the royal family look more like an American family, with Queen Victoria shorn of her tiara and Prince Albert shaved of his moustache. Within 20 years of this picture appearing, people were happily putting up Christmas trees in their homes all over America.

Christmas trees in American homes are often decorated with popcorn on a string, a leftover from the days when the tree was left outside and hung with fruit or nuts for the wild birds. Today trees are festooned with lights – the very first tree to be lit with electric lights belonged to Edward H. Johnson, a business associate of Thomas Edison, one of the early pioneers of the electric light bulb. Johnson had the idea of making lights specifically for the Christmas tree and ordered 80 small red, white and blue incandescent bulbs, which he draped across the tree in his house on Fifth Avenue in New York on 22 December 1882.

Perhaps the best-known Christmas tree in America is the Rockefeller Center Christmas tree in New York, first erected in 1933, although workers building the Center had put up their own small, unlit tree decorated with cranberries and ribbons of paper two years earlier in 1931. The Rockefeller tree is lit by the Mayor of New York City in late November in a public ceremony aired on NBC television's Christmas in Rockefeller Center. The tree, and the skating rink at its foot, which opened in 1936, are famous around the world, having appeared in countless Hollywood films.

America's National Christmas Tree stands in the grounds of the White House in Washington DC and has been lit by the President annually since 1923, when President Calvin Coolidge was the first to do the honours. The first Christmas tree to be seen *inside* the White House was erected in the 1850s during the presidency of Franklin Pierce, while President Benjamin Harrison put up a decorated tree in the Yellow Oval room in 1889 – and even dressed up as Santa Claus for the occasion. The first White House tree to have electric lights was paid for by President Grover Cleveland in 1895.

America's first public or communal illuminated Christmas tree was unveiled in Pasadena, California, in 1909, beginning a tradition that continues to this day.

Australia and New Zealand

The Christmas tree was brought to Australia by immigrants from Britain in the second half of the 19th century and trees are treated in just the same way there as they are in Britain. Since Christmas takes place in summer time in Australia and is often celebrated on the beach, trees are sometimes decorated with sea shells. Australia's first public tree was erected in Adelaide, but these days it is Melbourne's Federation Square that hosts the country's most spectacular tree.

In New Zealand the pohutukawa, a coastal evergreen with bright crimson flowers, has long been considered New Zealand's Christmas tree. The first known reference to the pohutukawa being used as a Christmas tree dates from 1857, when it was noted as a table decoration at a Christmas feast held by a Ngapuhi leader in the far north of North Island. The early European settlers seem to have adopted the pohutukawa right away and it became known as the Settler's Christmas Tree. Today it features in songs and on Christmas cards and serves as an iconic Christmas symbol for New Zealanders everywhere.

France

As Britain owes its first Christmas tree to Queen Charlotte of Mecklenburg, so it was also a lady from Mecklenburg, Duchess Helene Louise, who introduced the Christmas tree into France. In 1840, three years after she married the French aristocrat Ferdinand Philippe, Duke of Orleans, Duchess Helene had a tree put up in the Palace of the Tuileries in Paris. The custom wasn't picked up right away but the Christmas tree finally became a widely accepted part of Christmas celebrations in France with the arrival in the 1870s of refugees from the region of Alsace, who were displaced by the Franco-Prussian War. Alsace was originally part of the Germanic world where the Christmas tree had been popular since the 16th century. Today giant Christmas trees are erected in major towns across France, usually placed in front of the town's church or cathedral, as was the custom in northern Europe in the 15th and 16th centuries. Some 6 million Christmas trees are now sold in France every year. The most popular decorations are fruits, in particular red apples, chosen for their association with the apple from the Tree of Knowledge in the Garden of Eden. In 1858 there was a bad harvest caused by drought and apples were scarce, so people began using glass imitation apples instead and, more recently, chocolate apples.

Japan

Since Western influence on Japan grew, Christmas has been celebrated as a huge commercial occasion rather than a religious holiday. Some families have small Christmas trees in their homes and popular decorations include *mikan* (mandarin oranges), dolls, lanterns, wind chimes, paper fans and, a particular favourite with children, origami cranes. Osaka seems to be the city most committed to Christmas, with a large German Christmas market and a huge Christmas tree that for the past few years has won the Guinness World Record for 'Most lights on an artificial Christmas tree', boasting some 550,000 bulbs.

And now we've got the Christmas tree up, what are we going to put on it?

Deck the hall
with boughs of holly,

fa, la, la,
la, la, la,
la, la, la!

'Tis the season to be jolly,

fa, la, la,
la, la, la,
la, la, la!

During Advent, as well as putting up the tree, people bring down the dusty old cardboard box from the attic and get out the Christmas decorations.

Greenery

The first decorations of any kind were natural evergreens, which were used inside and outside by the ancient Egyptians, the Celts, the Vikings and other pre-Christian civilisations to celebrate the winter solstice, to ward off the evil spirits that proliferated in the dark winter months and to offer hope and encouragement that the warmth of the Sun would return after the cold of winter. During Saturnalia the Romans would deck their halls with boughs of holly and also send evergreen boughs to friends and acquaintances.

When the peoples of northern Europe began to celebrate Christmas instead of Saturnalia they continued the practice of decking out their halls and churches with evergreens, using the native evergreen plants that grew in abundance around them, such as holly, ivy and mistletoe. While the evergreens were still associated with growth and fertility they were imbued with a new, Christian meaning as well.

Cracker Joke
Knock knock!
Who's there?
Holly
Holly who?
—
Holly-days are
here again

Holly

Druids regarded holly, with its ability to thrive through the winter months, as a sacred or 'holy' plant. The origins of the words holly and holy are the same – holy (as in sacred) comes from the Old English word *halig*, meaning wholeness (holiness), a state of religious perfection, and halig in turn derives from an older word *holegn*, which is the Old English name for holly. The prickly leaves of the holly were thought to deter witches and demons and even malign elements such as thunder and lightning. To shield themselves from such abominations Druids would deck their temples with holly and, for added protection, they might even wear sprigs of holly in their hair when out and about.

For Christians, the prickle of the holly represents the crown of thorns as worn by Christ before he was nailed to the Cross, while the berries are stained forever red by the blood He shed.

The Christian symbolism is reflected in these lines from the traditional English carol 'The Holly and the Ivy', which dates from the 16th or 17th century. The form and music as we know them today are the work of folk music enthusiast Cecil J. Sharp, who collected and revived numerous old English folk songs and carols for his book *English Folk-Carols*, published in 1911.

The holly and the ivy,
When they are both full grown,
Of all the trees that are in the wood,
The holly bears the crown.

The holly bears a berry
As red as any blood ...

The holly bears a prickle
As sharp as any thorn ...

Holly and ivy were often linked together in a fertility context since pagans considered the hard, prickly holly to be a male plant and the softer ivy female, while for Christians the holly represents Christ and the ivy represents his mother, the Virgin Mary. Although it was considered unlucky to bring either plant into the house before Christmas Eve, it was said that whichever plant was discovered in the garden and brought indoors first would determine whether the man or woman of the house would be in charge that year!

Evergreen Wreaths

The word wreath comes from the Anglo-Saxon *wroeth* meaning
writhe or twist, but the use of wreaths made from evergreens
such as holly, laurel or pines goes back to far more ancient
times. Wreaths were worn as crowns by the Etruscans and then
by the ancient Greeks and the Romans to indicate status and
achievement. Victorious athletes at the original Olympic Games
were crowned with laurel wreaths. And, indeed, the circlet
crowns as worn ever since by European kings and queens are
really another form of wreath.

In a Christian context, the wreath proclaims Christ's victory over
death, while the circular shape of the wreath, with no beginning
or end, symbolises his promise of everlasting life. And a wreath
made of holly with its bright red berries must look very much like
the crown of thorns as worn by Jesus, dotted with red droplets of
blood from the bleeding wounds.

Wreaths have long been used as decoration for Christmas in both
Europe and America. In Britain, some people hang a wreath on
their front door during Advent to herald the Coming of Christ.
Others lay out a traditional Advent wreath set with candles that
are lit on each of the four Sundays in Advent.

Advent Wreath

The Advent wreath is a circle of evergreen plants, usually pine branches mixed with holly and perhaps mistletoe, that is laid somewhere in the home on a flat surface and set with four standing candles. Three purple and one pink, the candles represent the four Sundays of Advent. The first candle is lit on the first Sunday in Advent, and then two candles on the second Sunday, three on the third and all four on the fourth.

Sometimes there is a white candle symbolising purity which is placed in the middle of the wreath and lit on Christmas Eve. This is known as the Christ Candle and represents the life of Jesus Christ in the world.

The tradition of the Advent wreath comes, like so many Christmas traditions, from 16th-century Lutheran Germany, but the modern Advent wreath was the idea of a 19th-century German Protestant pastor called Johann Wichern, who designed it as a way of explaining Advent to the children of his mission school. Wichern's Advent wreath was made out of an old wooden wheel and had twenty small red candles and four large white candles. One small candle was lit on every weekday and Saturday during Advent and the four white candles were lit on the Sundays. Advent wreaths in Germany today still have red candles, although there are usually now only four of them.

Though popular in Germany since the 19th century, and in North America since the 1930s when they were introduced by German immigrants, Advent wreaths were not widely known in Britain until 1964, when the BBC children's programme *Blue Peter* demonstrated how to make an Advent wreath at home, inspiring a whole new generation to take up the idea.

Mistletoe

The name mistletoe comes from the Anglo-Saxon *mistel*, meaning mash or dung, and *tan* meaning twig. Mistletoe is actually a parasitic plant that feeds off other plants by attaching itself to a tree or shrub and then absorbing moisture and nutrients from its host.

Mistletoe seeds are spread by birds, such as the mistle thrush, which feed off the berries and discard the seeds, either through droppings or from their beak. The seed is covered by a sticky substance called viscin which then fastens the seed to the host.

So how did this mucky parasite become associated with kissing? Well, to begin with, the custom of kissing under the mistletoe seems to have started in England and spread from there to the rest of English-speaking world. This could either be because it has Druidical origins or because it comes down to us from our Norse ancestors.

There is certainly a Norse legend that could help explain it. The goddess Frigga (after whom Friday is named) was very protective of her son Baldur, the Sun god, and forced all things growing from the earth, be they rocks, plants or animals, to swear an oath not to harm him. A jealous rival to Baldur called Loki tricked Baldur's blind brother Hodur into shooting Baldur with an arrow made of mistletoe – the only thing that could have killed him because mistletoe never touches the ground and so doesn't grow from the earth. Distraught, Frigga wept, and as her tears fell on to the arrow they turned into beautiful white berries, with which she healed Baldur's wound and brought him back to life. She was so happy she blessed the mistletoe, granting all those who passed beneath it a kiss. There are other versions of this legend in which Baldur doesn't recover, but that doesn't fit the story we are trying to tell so we won't go there!

Then again, it could be the Druids who are responsible. The mistletoe flourishes while the host tree is without leaves and so the Druids thought it must have within it some mystical life force or fertility and, as with holly, they used it to ward off disease and evil spirits. Mistletoe grows particularly well on oak trees, which were worshipped by the Druids, and since it wrapped around the sacred oak tree and kept its spirit alive and warm during the winter they dedicated mistletoe to the goddess of love. Hence the mistletoe came to signify love and fertility.

Because it was a sacred plant there was, according to the Roman author and naturalist Pliny, quite a ritual to gathering in the mistletoe. It has no roots and in its natural state lives between the sky and the earth, never touching the ground, and so when collecting mistletoe it was important not to let it fall on to the

ground or it would lose its magical powers. The collecting Druid, dressed in a pure white robe, and possibly wearing a sprig of holly in his hair, would climb the tree and cut the mistletoe with a golden sickle while acolytes stood beneath with a white blanket to catch the sprigs as they fell. At the conclusion of the operation two white bulls would be sacrificed.

Some Christians tried to ban the mistletoe as a decoration in church because they didn't approve of this pagan love symbol. In the slightly more open-minded Britain of the 18th and 19th centuries, however, there was a great revival of interest in the Druids and their customs, and the idea of mistletoe as a potent fertility symbol was revisited.

Kissing under the mistletoe became a popular parlour game, particularly among the serving classes who were responsible for putting up the decorations in the Big House. Each white berry represented a kiss, and for each kiss given a berry was removed until none was left and the kissing had to stop. It was a modest echo, perhaps, of the licentious behaviour permitted during the old pagan or Roman festivals, and the fine old tradition of kissing under the mistletoe soon became widespread, along with other Christmas celebrations, under the Victorians.

Cracker Joke
What's green,
covered in tinsel
and goes ribbet
ribbet?

—

Mistle-toad!

Poinsettia

In more recent years, particularly in America, there is another plant, completely unrelated to pagan greenery, which thanks to its red and green leaves has become associated with Christmas, and that is the poinsettia. The plant comes from Mexico and was introduced to North America by the first US minister to Mexico, Joel Roberts Poinsett, in the 1820s. Poinsettias are everywhere in America at Christmas-time now and are becoming more and more popular in Britain, even though they are notoriously difficult to look after.

Cracker Joke
What do you get if you cross a Christmas tree with an apple?
—
A pineapple

Decorations and Ornaments for the Christmas tree

The first tree ornaments were natural growing things such as pine cones, berries and nuts, or fruits such as the apples that were hung from the fir trees used to represent the Tree of Knowledge of Good and Evil in the Paradise Plays.

The first ornaments we know about that were used specifically on Christmas trees were the fruits, nuts and baked goods hung on the Christmas tree in Freiburg in 1419 (see Chapter 2), while the tree put up in Riga in 1510 was garlanded with paper roses – roses being associated with the Virgin Mary.

As we have seen, it may have been Martin Luther who was the first person to take a fir tree indoors and put candles on it, but the first written record we have of indoor decorated Christmas trees comes from a German chronicler in 1605 who wrote about the people of Strasbourg (then in Germany) who would put up trees in their parlours and

> 'hang thereon roses cut out of paper of many colours, apples, wafers, spangle-gold and sugar ...'

Fruit wasn't always easy to procure and people started to design and make their own Christmas tree decorations using paper flowers and stars, painted eggshells, ribbons, small wooden toys, various kinds of foods such as biscuits, sweets and nuts, anything they could think of to brighten up the tree. Many ornaments were symbolic of something – walnuts, for instance, were considered by the Romans to be 'the nut of the gods' and have always been associated with good health. Birds are a universal symbol of happiness, doves in particular representing peace and love and in Christianity symbolising the Holy Spirit.

Acorns are a good luck symbol as they come from the sacred oak tree. In Christianity they represent new life as personified in the birth of Jesus.

Pickles are also a symbol of good luck. In some countries the pickle is the last ornament to be hung and is hidden among the boughs of the tree – and the first child to find it is given a special treat.

Tinsel

In 1610, Christmas tree decoration took a great leap forward when what we know as tinsel was invented in Nuremberg in Germany. Although tinsel sounds like a German word, it is actually known in Germany as *lametta*, from the Italian word *lama*, meaning blade, and was designed to replicate icicles hanging from the tree. Our word tinsel comes from the French *étincelle*, meaning sparkle, which is precisely what tinsel does when draped around the room or across the tree, enhancing and reflecting the light of the flickering candles.

Cracker Joke
What do you get
if you eat Christmas
decorations?

—

Tinselitus

Nuremberg was renowned for its silverware and the first tinsel was made from very thin strips of real silver, a fortunate side product of silver making. The problem with real silver, though, was that while it was durable it quickly became tarnished by the smoke from the candles. So all sorts of other materials were tried, including aluminium, pewter, tin and eventually lead foil, which was marvellous as it gave the tinsel weight, didn't tarnish and remained shiny. However, in the 1960s, the authorities began to worry about lead poisoning and manufacturers were advised to switch to lighter plastic materials for their tinsel. Plastic, alas, didn't hang so well but at least it was safe. Today tinsel is manufactured in many countries, mostly made from PVC with a metallic finish, and it comes in all colours, not just silver. It is still possible to buy real silver tinsel from Germany – at a cost – and with plastics now becoming an environmental issue we might all have to go back to real silver for our tinsel before too long.

Glass Ornaments: Birth of the Bauble

The birthplace of the traditional Christmas bauble is the small German town of Lauscha in eastern Germany. The town's location in a forest upon a limestone upland provides all the ingredients for glass making: sand from the limestone and timber for potash and for firing the glass ovens. In the late 16th century, around 1595, two craftsmen, Hans Greiner and Christoff Mueller, set up Germany's first glassworks at Lauscha with a licence from the Duke of Saxe-Coburg. Their glassware became so popular that other glassworks sprang up around them and Lauscha developed into Germany's pre-eminent glass making centre. As well as producing drinking glasses, flasks and bowls, Greiner and Mueller became famous for their garlands of glass beads which were used for decorating Christmas trees. Like tinsel, they twinkled in the candlelight; unlike tinsel, they didn't tarnish. Thanks to Greiner and Mueller, Lauscha soon acquired a reputation as the place to go to for Christmas ornaments.

In the early 19th century, another Hans Greiner, a descendant of the first, started to create glass ornaments in the shape of fruits and nuts, trumpets, angels, stars and even Santas, by inserting a glass tube into a clay mould and blowing the heated glass into the shape of the mould. He then went on to design glass baubles, and using a silvering technique developed by a German chemist called Justus von Liebig (who would go on to give us Oxo cubes and, indirectly, Marmite), he discovered he was able to line the inside of the bauble with a silver nitrate solution to give it a nice silvery look. The outside of the shiny bauble was then coated with a coloured dye and a thin metal cap fixed to the top along with a loop with which to tie it on to the tree. The first written record of one of these glass baubles, which in Germany are called *Kugeln*, appears in 1848.

Queen Victoria's husband Prince Albert, whose Saxe-Coburg ancestor had sponsored the first Hans Greiner, imported glass ornaments from Lauscha into England for the royal Christmas tree at Windsor, and after the tree appeared in the *Illustrated London News*, demand for these ornaments, and for the pretty new glass baubles, soared. The glass makers of Lauscha found themselves working flat out to increase production of Christmas ornaments for export all over Europe.

Then, in 1880, during a trip to Germany, the American entrepreneur F. W. Woolworth came across the glassworks at Lauscha and took some sample Christmas ornaments home to America, where he put them on sale in his store in Pennsylvania. Within ten years he was selling millions of them.

Lauscha continued to produce handmade Christmas ornaments until after the Second World War, when the Iron Curtain fell across Germany, trapping the village in the Communist East. Christmas baubles, it seems, were not a priority for the Communists who took over the glassworks. Firms in America, Japan and the Czech Republic took up the slack and millions of Christmas ornaments are now mass produced across the world.

For handmade Christmas ornaments, however, Germany is once more the place to go. When the Berlin Wall came down in 1989 the glassworks in Lauscha that had survived the Communists became private companies again, and today there are some twenty small glass making firms there producing Christmas ornaments. Now every December Lauscha holds its own Christmas market where people from around the world can come and see demonstrations of glass blowing and browse Lauscha's boutiques with their huge selection of handmade glass ornaments and baubles. The site of Hans Greiner and Christoff Mueller's original workshop in Lauscha can be found at the central square called the Hüttenplatz, meaning 'foundry place'.

The Top of the Tree

Perhaps the most important Christmas tree decoration of them all is the one that goes on the top of the tree. Originally it was a lighted candle, but safety concerns have long since put a stop to that. Today it is most likely to be a star, representing the Star of Bethlehem, or an angel, representing the Angel of the Lord who brought the glad tidings of Jesus' birth to the shepherds keeping watch over their flock by night.

The Star of Bethlehem

The Star of Bethlehem is the star that led the wise men,
or Magi, to Bethlehem where the newborn Christ Child was
lying in a manger.

'And lo, the star which they saw
in the east went before them,
till it came and stood over where
the young child was. And when
they saw the star, they rejoiced
with exceeding great joy.'

Matthew, Chapter 2, verses 9–10

For many Christians that is all they need to know. Others of
a more scientific or curious bent have sought to explain the
star – which is not easy.

There are conflicting theories among Bible scholars as to the
actual nature of the star. Some think it was a comet, others
that it might have been a conjunction of planets, while still
more wonder if it might not have been light from the birth
of a new star, known as a nova. Unfortunately, none of these
explanations will quite suffice. To begin with the text implies
that only the wise men saw the star – if it was a natural
phenomenon, then why did nobody else see it? Another
complication is that, due to the rotation of the Earth, celestial
bodies normally move from east to west across the heavens,
and yet the Star of Bethlehem led the Three Kings south from
Jerusalem to Bethlehem after they had met with King Herod.
And then it stood still right over the place where Jesus lay.
Hmm. Nevertheless, however it got there, a star on the top of
the Christmas tree signals the birth of Jesus and his presence
in the home.

While we are here, talking about the Star of Bethlehem, it
might be a good time to talk about the wise men, since they are
important members of the cast in the story of the Nativity.

We three kings of Orient are
Bearing gifts we traverse afar
Field and fountain, moor and mountain
Following yonder star

O star of wonder, star of night
Star with royal beauty bright
Westward leading, still proceeding
Guide us to thy Perfect Light

St Luke doesn't say anything about wise men, it is only St Matthew who mentions them in his Gospel and he doesn't tell us very much, certainly not that there were three of them '... behold, wise men from the east came to Jerusalem.'

The reason we suppose there were three of them is because they gave Jesus the three gifts of gold, frankincense and myrrh. Likewise, Matthew says nothing about them being kings, but he does say that they 'fell down and worshipped Jesus when they saw him', and since there are Old Testament prophecies in the Psalms predicting that 'all kings shall fall down before him', so it is possible to see how people might have thought them to be kings. Finally, they are sometimes referred to as 'Magi' because they came from the east and Magi were members of a priestly caste, or wise men, from Persia, in the east.

Although the wise men often appear in cribs and Nativity scenes they were not there on the night of Jesus' birth. No one is quite sure when they did visit Jesus, but convention says they it was on Epiphany, 6 January.

But let's get back to the top of the tree.

The Angel of the Lord

'And an angel of the Lord stood before them, and the glory of the Lord shone around them, and they were sore afraid. And the angel said to them, 'Be not afraid; for behold I bring you good tidings of great joy which shall be to all people. For there is born to you this day in the city of David a Saviour, which is Christ the Lord.'

Luke, Chapter 2, verses 8–11

Angels play many roles in Christianity but are perhaps most commonly thought of either as guardians or as messengers of God, and it is in this latter capacity that angels appear in the Christmas story. The Angel Gabriel appears to the Virgin Mary to tell her that she will conceive a son, and later an unnamed angel of the Lord comes to bring the news of Jesus' birth to the shepherds watching their flock by night. Hence an angel on the top of the Christmas tree heralds the news of Jesus' birth as well as guarding the home from evil spirits, much as holly once did for pagans.

Now we'll examine some more of the things we get up to during Advent.

Cracker Joke
What happened
to the man who
stole an Advent
Calendar?

—

He got 24 days!

A bit like the Advent wreath, the Advent calendar provides a way of counting down to Christmas, and again like the wreath, it comes to us from Germany.

The traditional Advent calendar is a large rectangular sheet of paper or cardboard showing a Christmas scene in which there are doors or windows numbered 1 to 24, one for each day of December up to and including 24 December (Christmas Eve). Each day the door numbered with that day's date is opened to reveal a picture from the Nativity story or a verse from the Bible, or a treat such as a toy or a chocolate.

It was Protestants in 19th-century Germany who first had the idea of finding ways of counting down the days to Christmas, no doubt to keep their expectant children quiet while they were waiting impatiently through the dark December days for the fun to begin. One way to count down was to make chalk marks on a door which could then be wiped out one by one. Another way was to light a candle each day, like on the first Advent wreaths. Sometimes the candles would be placed on to a special Christmas tree where the effect of the ever-increasing display of lights reflected the approach of Jesus, Light of the World. Some parents made Christmas clocks with round faces divided into 24 segments on which the hands could be moved one step each day.

The Advent calendar as we know it today was pioneered by a German publisher and printer from Maulbronn called Gerhard Lang (1881–1974), who took his inspiration from something his mother thought up for him when he was a child. She took an ordinary cardboard calendar, laid it down on a table and placed a type of cookie called a *Wibele* on each of the December days up to the 24th, and every day the young Gerhard would get to remove a Wibele and eat it. Developing this idea, in 1904 Lang produced a Christmas calendar (*Weihnachts-Kalender*) as an insert for the *Stuttgarter Zeitung* newspaper. It consisted of two parts, a cardboard calendar page with 24 boxes containing the date and a poem for each day, and a printed sheet of 24 pictures to cut out each day and stick in one of the boxes. For the 24th day there was a picture of the Christ Child dressed all in white.

Next Lang refined his calendars by adding the little doors or windows that are the main feature we associate with Advent calendars today. In 1908 he produced the first commercial, mass-produced Advent calendars and sales soared. Other manufacturers copied the idea and within a few years Advent calendars were being put up in homes all across Germany.

With mass production, however, came a problem. Advent was officially supposed to start on the fourth Sunday before Christmas, but this fell on a different date every year. As a result the Advent calendar had to be redesigned every year, a costly and time-consuming process. So Lang decided that his calendars would always start on 1 December. Other manufacturers followed suit and now all but bespoke Advent calendars run from 1 December.

Gerhard Lang went out of business in 1940, partly because of a cardboard shortage caused by the Second World War and partly because the high quality and attention to detail of his calendars made them too expensive, even when mass produced.

After the war, in 1945, another German publisher, Richard Sellmar of Stuttgart, designed a handmade Advent calendar with the motif 'The Little Christmas Town'. This featured a row of assorted town buildings with windows that opened to show pictures of various characters engaged in Christmas activities relevant to the particular building. Sellmar set up his own firm and in 1946 began printing the calendar for sale. It proved very popular, particularly with the Americans who were running Stuttgart at the time, and in the 1950s a picture appeared in the American newspapers of President Eisenhower's three grandchildren posing with a 'Little Christmas Town' Advent calendar that was being sold to raise funds for the National Epilepsy League. The Advent calendar took off in America and Richard Sellmar's firm has since grown into one of the biggest producers of Advent calendars in the world, selling millions of calendars every year in a variety of motifs, themes and formats, including a yearly Advent calendar featuring the White House for the US President.

Advent calendars are no longer exclusively religious. Today there are Advent calendars of all shapes and sizes and themes, featuring all kinds of different items behind the windows and designed not just for domestic use but for all sorts of commercial purposes from advertising to fund raising. The first Advent calendars containing chocolates were produced in 1958, with the famous Cadbury's chocolate calendar first appearing in 1971. LEGO produces an Advent calendar set. There are calendars filled with alcoholic treats, beauty products, souvenirs from TV and film franchises, DIY products, small electronic items, treats for dogs, cats and horses, tea bags and even different cheeses, which must smell like old socks by Christmas Eve – a useful reminder to put out the Christmas stockings, perhaps?

Some German towns even kit out whole buildings as Advent calendars. Every year, for instance, the picturesque 18th-century pink stone *Rathaus*, or town hall, of the beautiful half-timbered town of Gengenbach in the Black Forest region of south-west Germany is transformed into what they like to think is the world's largest Advent calendar. Its 24 windows facing the town square are decorated with Christmas scenes which are revealed and lit up one by one every night until Christmas.

The world record for the largest Advent calendar actually goes to St Pancras Station in London. In 2007 a giant calendar 233 feet (71 m) high and 75 feet (23 m) wide was constructed on the back wall of the station to celebrate its refurbishment. Local retailers sponsored the windows and every day a different event was held to mark the opening of each calendar window.

In the Nordic countries – Norway, Sweden, Finland, Denmark and Iceland – the Advent calendar, or *Julkalendar*, can take the form of a radio or television show with 24 episodes. Episode one is broadcast on the evening of 1 December and then another episode each night until the climax on 24 December, Christmas Eve. The idea came from Sweden, where the first such Julkalendar was broadcast on Swedish radio in 1957, and the first television version was shown on Swedish television in 1960.

The Advent calendar certainly has come a long way since Mother Lang's little *Wibele*.

Cracker Joke
Why is it getting harder to buy Advent calendars?

—

Because their days are numbered!

Christmas Cards

The writing and sending of Christmas cards is, perhaps, the most time-consuming of all Advent customs, and yet it was in order to save time and effort that Victorian civil servant Sir Henry Cole (1808–1882) came up with the idea of the Christmas card in the first place.

Henry Cole was an extraordinary man. In pursuit of his stated goal to 'beautify life' he was a children's author, a designer of tea pots for Minton, a commissioner for the Great Exhibition of 1851, the first director of the Victoria and Albert Museum and a leading light in establishing the Royal College of Art, the Royal College of Music and Imperial College, London. But it is his role in introducing the world's first universal postal service in 1840 that concerns us here. From 1837 until 1840 Henry Cole worked with Rowland Hill to establish the Penny Post, whereby a letter could be posted to anywhere in the UK for a penny. The postage could be prepaid by the sender with the world's first postage stamp, the Penny Black, which Henry Cole is believed to have designed himself.

The result of the introduction of the Penny Post, which Henry Cole promoted enthusiastically among his wide circle of friends, was that his wide circle of friends all began to send letters to each other, particularly at Christmas-time when they would send long, rambling festive greetings that demanded a reply.

As we can see, Henry Cole was a busy man and replying to all this correspondence became too much. But, on the other hand, he didn't want to be rude. So instead he devised a way by which he could answer all his friends and acquaintances at the same time in a manner calculated to delight and amuse. To begin with, he asked an artist friend of his, John Calcott Horsley, to design an illustration based on an idea that Cole had in his mind. Horsley went home to his studio at Orestone Manor in Devon and emerged some days later with paint on his nose and an enchanting hand-coloured picture, showing a family celebrating Christmas flanked by charitable figures caring for the less fortunate, along with the salutation 'A Merry Christmas and a Happy New Year To You'. At the top was the word 'To', followed by a line on which to write the name of the recipient, and at the bottom was the word 'From', where Henry Cole could sign his own name. The image was printed on a sheet of cardboard and, lo and behold, there was the world's first Christmas card. Henry Cole had 1,000 printed off, sent most of them to his friends and sold the rest for one shilling each for charity – the first charity cards.

The cards were well received by almost everyone, although there were a few Temperance eyebrows raised as the illustration showed a child apparently being offered a sip of wine, an outrage that, in

this stern day and age, would have seen Henry Cole denounced
and the card banned from all reputable card shops.

Of course, as soon as you ban something it becomes all the more
sought after, and in 2001 one of Henry Cole's twelve surviving
original Christmas cards, the one sent to his grandmother, in fact,
sold at auction for a world record £22,500. A good incentive,
surely, to remember to send a Christmas card to your granny.

At first, Christmas cards were the preserve of the rich – a penny
was a day's wage for the average working man. However, as the
railway network developed, it gradually became easier to transport
letters all across the country quickly and in bulk, and in 1870 the
price of a stamp came down to a more affordable halfpenny. Not
long after that, thanks to improvements in printing technology,
the printing firm of Prang & Mayer started to mass produce
Christmas cards in London, and they were soon followed by
playing card manufacturers such as Charles Goodall & Son and
Thomas De La Rue. By 1880 some 12 million cards had been sold
in Britain.

In 1875, Louis Prang of Prang & Mayer introduced the Christmas
card to America and before long he was producing more than
5 million cards a year for the US market.

In 1891, while she was staying in Glasgow in Scotland, the
sharpshooter Annie Oakley, star of Buffalo Bill's Wild West Show,
sent the first personalised Christmas card on record to her friends
and family back in the USA. The card included a photo of Annie
dressed, appropriately, in tartan.

In 1916, jobbing printer Joyce Hall and his brothers Rollie and
William formed The Hall Brothers Company and began printing
Christmas cards at their works in Kansas City, Missouri. They
decided not to use the traditional postcard format but came up
with a new design, a card folded once and placed in an envelope.
This design, just the right size for those who didn't need to write
a whole letter, became the standard format for greetings cards.
Hall Brothers changed their name to Hallmark and the modern
Christmas card was born.

Christmas cards today are very different to Henry Cole's bucolic
family scene of 1843. The early Victorian cards tended to be
simple and secular, a bit like visiting cards, with pictures of
evergreen flowers and plants indicating the arrival of spring, or
sentimental images of children or slightly questionable depictions
of animals dressed up as humans. Different times, I suppose. Then
printing methods got more sophisticated and it became possible
to illustrate more suitable religious themes such as Madonna
and Child, angels, cherubs and scenes from the Nativity. And, as

Prince Albert and Charles Dickens began to shape the modern Christmas, so the familiar Christmas symbols began to appear on the cards: Christmas trees, holly, snow scenes, Christmas puddings, carol singers, Father Christmas, doves and robins.

Robins? Why do robins appear on Christmas cards? Well, because of their red uniforms, Victorian postmen were nicknamed 'robins' and it was only natural that real robins began to appear on Christmas cards to symbolise the postman delivering the Christmas post. But even apart from that, robins have always held a special place in the heart of the British public. In many other countries, robins are hunted and consequently are very shy, but in Britain they are the gardener's constant companion, even coming into the home sometimes. I remember when I was a boy growing up in Devon my father's most loyal friend was a robin called Arnold, who would not only pose for us by perching on the handle of the garden spade but would come into the kitchen and join us at the breakfast table. For a Briton, killing a robin, the herald of spring, was and still is, considered unlucky. And so, instead, we made the robin the National Bird of Britain. And an enduring symbol of Christmas.

Incidentally, do you know how the robin got its red breast? Well, the story goes that when Mary was resting in the stable in Bethlehem the fire that was keeping her and the baby Jesus warm began to die. A little brown bird in the eves saw what was happening and flew down to the fire and flapped its wings like a pair of bellows until the dying embers burst into flames again, scorching its brown breast red. Mary blessed the robin for what its had done and said, 'Let your red breast for ever be a reminder of your kind deed this night.'

As Christmas cards became more popular, competitions were held to find new designs and ideas. The best illustrators were commissioned to create new scenes, and the best writers were hired to compose new verses and greetings. A new art form emerged and Christmas cards became collector's items, just like stamps.

Speaking of stamps, the first Christmas stamp was a Canadian stamp marked 'Xmas 1898', issued to commemorate the inauguration of the Imperial Penny Postage rate on Christmas Day 1898. It has been argued that, since the stamp was not issued expressly for Christmas, this is not really the first Christmas stamp, but it is the first stamp ever to mention Christmas and that is good enough for me. Various stamps with Christmas scenes were issued in Austria, Brazil and Hungary in the 1930s and 40s but the first set of specifically Christmas stamps issued as part of what became an annual tradition were issued in Australia in 1957. The first US Christmas stamps appeared in 1962, the first UK Christmas stamps not until 1966.

The practice of sending official Christmas cards was begun by Queen Victoria in 1840, after her marriage to Prince Albert. For Christmas that year she sent an engraving of Christmas celebrations at Windsor to various friends and members of her household and government, a tradition that has been maintained by the royal family ever since.

The first official White House Christmas card was sent by US President Eisenhower in 1953 to some 500 people. Today the card, which traditionally shows White House scenes painted by renowned American artists, is sent to around one and a half million people.

Cracker Joke
What did the stamp say to the Christmas card?

—

Stick with me and we'll go places!

Today, between 700 and 900 million Christmas cards are sent in Britain every year, while in America anything up to 2 billion Christmas cards are sent. In the UK some £50 million is raised by the sale of charity cards each year. Little did Sir Henry Cole know what he was starting …

Now read on if you want to learn about the activity that really means Christmas for people all over the world – shopping.

For many people Christmas shopping is bliss. For others it is misery. But there is one form of Christmas shopping that everyone can enjoy. Christmas markets.

Think of a Christmas market and you can't help but think of Germany, for that is where Christmas markets, or *Weihnachtsmärkte* as they are called in Germany, originated, and that is still where the best Christmas markets are found.

The Christmas markets that today usher in Advent grew out of the winter markets that were held in many German towns and cities in the 13th and 14th centuries. These markets were held for one or two days to give people an opportunity to stock up on food and supplies for the cold winter months ahead. The first such winter market for which we have a record is Vienna's Dezembermarkt of 1296, when the city's shopkeepers were granted the right to hold a two-day market by Duke Albrecht I.

Winter markets became more than just a chance to stock up; they were a good opportunity for people to meet up and enjoy a chat and a drink together, and over time, in addition to the stalls of the shopkeepers, food stalls sprang up to provide goodies such as roasted almonds and chestnuts, gingerbread and sweets. Local craftsmen, too, set up stalls to sell their toys and woodworks. Many of these items were bought as presents for children, and in 1310 a forerunner to the Christmas market was held in Munich that acquired the name *Nikolausdult*, after St Nicholas, the traditional giver of presents in Germany. At that time presents were given out on St Nicholas' Day, 6 December, and so the market had nothing to do with Christmas. Other winter markets that involved some elements of Christmas but could not yet be called true Christmas markets were held in Bautzen, in what is now eastern Germany, in 1384, and Frankfurt am Main in 1393.

The Birthplace of Stollen

The world's first official Christmas market was the one-day *Striezelmarkt* held in Dresden in 1434 by kind permission of Frederick II, the Elector of Saxony. The Striezelmarkt was actually a meat market where the people of the town could purchase the meat for their Christmas meal, but it was named after a local delicacy called *Striezel*, which is the Saxon name for Stollen, a delicacy for which Dresden was, and is, famous. Dresden's Christmas Stollen, or Christstollen, was first mentioned in 1474 on the bill of fare at Dresden's St Bartholomew's Hospital, although it is known to have been baked in Dresden long before that. This original Stollen was a very abstemious affair made from nothing but yeast, flour and water. There was no butter or milk, because the Catholic Church frowned upon the use of such decadent pleasures during Advent. The good people of Saxony didn't think much of this and petitioned the Pope to revoke the butter ban, which he did in 1491. The bakers of Dresden Christstollen were then able to produce something more like the delicious treat we know and love today. A moist fruit bread of nuts, spices and dried fruit sprinkled with icing sugar, Stollen has become a favourite Christmas indulgence world-wide in recent years and Dresden's Stollen is considered to be the best.

Cracker Joke
Why couldn't they find the Christmas cake?
—
Because it was stollen!

The city's famous *Stollenfest* has been celebrated since the 15th century, and although it was halted for much of the 20th century by two world wars, it was started up again in 1994 and now goes from strength to strength. Held on the Saturday before the second Sunday in Advent the festival sees a huge Stollen, weighing three or four tons, paraded through the streets of Dresden on a carriage. When it arrives at the Christmas market, the Stollen is shared out amongst the crowd, having been divided up by the *Stollenmadchen*, Dresden's version of a Christmas beauty queen, using the Grand Dresden Stollen Knife.

Christkindlesmärkte

In the middle of the 16th century, the Protestant reformer Martin Luther, who disapproved of the veneration of the Catholic St Nicholas, decided to introduce a new present-giving practice. In place of St Nicholas he introduced the Christkind or Christ Child, an incarnation of the baby Jesus, as the giver of gifts, and changed the day of gift giving from St Nicholas's Day, 6 December, to Christmas Eve, 24 December. In this way, people's thoughts would be drawn to the true meaning of Christmas as a celebration of the birth of Christ. This idea was taken up by more and more Christmas markets, especially those in Bavaria and the south of Germany, and they started to call themselves *Christkindlesmärkte*, or Christ Child Markets.

The first market officially to call itself a *Christkindlesmarkt*, and now the most celebrated Christmas market of them all, is the Nuremberg Christkindlesmarkt, for which the earliest record is 1628, although there is some evidence that it was behaving in the manner of a Christkindlesmarkt as far back as 1564.

Today the opening ceremony of the Nuremberg Christkindlesmarkt takes place on the Friday before Advent during which the Christ Child, represented by a specially chosen local girl in her late teens, reads out the Prologue of the Christ Child from the balcony of the Frauenkirche in the main square and then declares the market open. Over 2 million people now visit the colourful, authentically old-fashioned 'little town of wood and canvas' that fills the heart of Nuremberg's Old Town every year. Among the delights for them to enjoy are *Zwetschgenmännle* (figures made from prunes), *Nürnberger Rostbratwürste* (a type of small sausage served with sauerkraut), *Lebkuchen* (gingerbread) and numerous other local specialities along with a crib, Christmas lights, traditional handmade toys, Christmas tree decorations and ornaments, and a glass or two of mulled wine.

The first Christmas markets usually lasted for no more than two or three days, whereas today's Christmas markets are really Advent markets and can run for anything between two and four weeks. Every one of Germany's Christmas markets has its own distinctive flavour and specialities, selling local delicacies along with crafts and ornaments made in the surrounding region, a characteristic inherited from the days when only local traders were allowed to sell their wares at the town's market. An aficionado deposited in a German Christmas market would pretty soon be able to tell you where the market is by the food and wares on sale there. In essence, Germany's Christmas markets have not changed for centuries and still today provide a place for locals and visitors alike to meet up and enjoy the festive season together, while perhaps sampling a festive brew or two and browsing through the homemade produce and locally made Christmas goods.

We may think that it is only in modern times that Christmas has become rampant with consumerism, but right up until the middle of the 19th century, when people like the department store magnate F. W. Woolworth came along, Christmas markets were the only places where people could buy everything they needed for Christmas, and they have been enticing people away from more devout pursuits for centuries. Markets were originally held in front of the church as a way of encouraging people to attend service, but the lure of retail therapy proved too strong even in more pious times – in 1616 the priest of Nuremberg's Frauenkirche complained that nobody came to church on Christmas Eve because they were all too busy shopping at the market instead!

Christmas Markets around the World

Christmas markets can now be found in many countries across the world, although none can quite match the German markets. Some of the best markets in Europe outside Germany include Prague, in the Czech Republic, held in the Christmassy-sounding Wenceslas Square, the atmospheric old towns of Wroclaw and Krakow in Poland, Vienna and Salzburg in Austria, both of which date back to the 15th century, Riga in Latvia, which goes back even further, Tallinn in Estonia, where you can shop until 7 January, which is Christmas Day for the Russian Orthodox Church, and Zurich in Switzerland, which packs out the biggest covered market in Europe.

Gothenburg holds Sweden's biggest Christmas market, while the one held in Copenhagen's Tivoli Gardens is Denmark's favourite market. And, of course, there is the very special Christmas market held at Santa Claus' home up in the Arctic Circle at Rovaniemi in Lapland.

The first Christmas market in Britain was held in Manchester in 1999 with just 15 stalls. Today the number of stalls has risen to over 300, making it Britain's biggest Christmas market, and more than nine million people visit every year. The biggest authentic German Christmas market in Britain is Birmingham's Frankfurt Christmas Market which began in 2001 with 24 stalls and now boasts 180 stalls and five and a half million visitors. This is also the biggest authentic German Christmas market anywhere in the world outside of Germany and Austria.

Chicago boasts what is generally regarded as America's most authentic Christmas market, while Canada's most traditional one is held in Kitchener, South Ontario, home of the country's oldest and largest German community. Russia's premier Christmas market is held in St Petersburg while the Christmas market in Tokyo's Hibiya Park, part sponsored by the German Tourism Association, boasts hot sake and a 50-foot- (15-metre-) high wooden Christmas pyramid imported from the woodcraft centre of Seiffen in Germany.

Although the warmer countries of southern Europe and many of those in the southern hemisphere try hard to create their own Christmas markets they can't really compete – a real Christmas market requires winter weather and, ideally, snow. Still, one year it might be nice to trade a grey December sky for some Aussie warmth and try the Hahndorf Christkindlesmarkt near Adelaide in South Australia, which has a good pedigree – Hahndorf is Australia's oldest German settlement.

Next we will look at another Advent tradition, the Nativity play.

'For it is in giving that we receive.'
St Francis of Assisi

In Christian countries, during Advent, many schools and church communities put on Nativity plays which recreate the story of the birth of Jesus.

The first performance of what might be described as a Nativity play was put on for the townspeople of Greccio in Italy in 1223 by St Francis of Assisi, who officiated at a midnight mass staged in a cave beneath the convent in front of a life-size Nativity scene. St Francis had been inspired by a visit to the site of Jesus' birth in Bethlehem and wanted to recreate for his followers how it might have looked, with Jesus lying in a manger while the ox and ass looked on.

St Francis went on to produce many more Nativity plays, the intention behind them being not just to illustrate the birth of Jesus in a way that ordinary people could grasp and appreciate, but to show how Jesus was born into a life of poverty and simplicity, much like their own lives. The idea spread throughout Europe and gradually the Latin chants of the original mass were replaced with new songs and carols sung in the local vernacular so that they could be understood by everybody watching.

Over time, more characters from the Nativity were added, such as the shepherds with their crooks and the wise men, even though in real life these different characters were never all present in the stable at the same time.

In the Nativity plays put on by churches and schools today the characters, even the ox and ass, are played by children. Sometimes the baby Jesus is a real baby, although it is not always easy to find a parent who is willing to hand over their beloved infant to a five-year-old Mary, and if this is the case the baby Jesus can be played by a doll. And occasionally, as a special treat, a well-meaning clergyman or teacher will decide to cast a real animal, usually a donkey, in the role of ass, an injudicious move that has been known to result in some memorable scenes of chaos and disaster. As the saying goes; never work with children and animals.

Cribs

A crib is a tableau of the Nativity scene and usually consists of a stable with, at its centre, a manger full of straw in which the baby Jesus is laid (a manger is a trough from which animals feed). The regular characters include Mary and Joseph and an ox and ass, to which may be added the shepherds with their crooks and maybe a sheep or two, the three wise men with their gifts of gold, frankincense and myrrh, and possibly some angels. Cribs can also be found at Christmas markets, in town squares and shop windows, and in some homes during Advent.

The first live crib was the one displayed in the cave for St Francis of Assisi's special midnight mass held in Greccio in 1223. It was designed and put together by a local nobleman and follower of St Francis called Giovanni Velita. He used a large stone with some straw on it for the manger and laid a carved image of Jesus on top of the straw. And he borrowed a live ox and ass from a nearby farmer to stand by the manger and gaze at the baby Jesus while serenely chewing the cud.

Although Giovanni Velita's tableau was the first known *live* crib, it was not the first crib. That honour goes to the Italian city of Naples, where a crib was documented as early as 1025 in a long lost Church of St Maria del Presepe (St Mary of the Crib). In Naples a crib is known as a *presepe* and a crib made in Naples is a Presepe Napoletano – these are considered the finest cribs in the world, not least by the Neopolitans themselves. Neopolitan *presepi* consist of much more than the traditional Nativity scene of the baby Jesus, Mary and Joseph and the ox and ass. Sometimes a whole village is built around the manger with running water, twinkling lights and a cast of villagers. In fact the largest Nativity scene in the world can be seen in Naples in the Museo Nazionale di San Martino, housed in a former monastery. Known as the Presepe Cuciniello, the crib includes more than 160 characters, with 28 angels, some 80 animals, and over 400 objects.

Most Neopolitan presepi are made in the workshops that line both sides of the Via San Gregorio Armeno, a pedestrianised street known as Christmas Alley. Here you can observe craftsmen busy carving and painting Nativity scenes and characters all year round.

The world's oldest surviving crib can be seen in the museum of the Basilica of St Maria Maggiore in Rome. The basilica was built in about AD 420 on the site of an older church, and and few years later, in AD 432, the new Pope, Sixtus III, constructed an underground chapel inside the church replicating the 'cave of the Nativity' in Bethlehem where Jesus was thought to have been born. Sixtus filled it with relics from the original Holy Crib that were brought to Rome by pilgrims returning from the Holy Land including, it is said, fragments of the actual manger where Jesus 'lay down his sweet head' and cloth from his swaddling clothes. Later, in 1288, Pope Nicolo IV commissioned the Tuscan sculptor Arnolfo di Cambio to complete the scene by sculpting a crib for the chapel, comprising the figures of the Virgin Mary and the baby Jesus, Joseph, the three wise men and the ox and ass. It seems that the sculpture of the Virgin Mary was lost and replaced by another Mary some 300 years later, but the other figurines of the world's oldest Nativity scene survive and can be seen in the museum. The underground chapel of the 'cave of the Nativity' is still there in the basilica and contains a silver reliquary holding the wood from the Holy Manger.

Now for that most evocative of Advent traditions – Christmas music.

Christmas would not be Christmas without the familiar hymns and carols and jingles and songs and chorales that fill the spirit with Christmas cheer and instantly evoke images of flickering candles, roaring log fires, angels, the ox and the ass and children gathered around the baby in a manger, mince pies and mulled wine, presents under the tree, a star in the east, family.

Carols

The singing of carols, songs and hymns that tell the story of Christmas and the Nativity is a tradition that goes back almost to the birth of Christ itself, but the roots of carol singing go back even further.

Carol singing has its origins in the old practice of wassailing, which itself evolved from the pagan custom of offering up songs and sacrifices in midwinter for the good health of the coming harvest.

The word 'wassail' comes from the Saxon weas hael meaning 'be of good health'. This was the toast given by the Saxon lord of the manor to his people at the start of the new year, to which the people would reply *drink hael*, or 'drink well', and all would drink from a huge wassail bowl passed around from person to person with a traditional wassail greeting. Depending on where in the country you were, the wassail drink would be made up from warm ale, wine or cider mixed with honey, spices, eggs and cream with little pieces of toast floating on the top.

In the countryside, after dark on Twelfth Night, 5 January, or Old Twelvey Night, 17 January, if using the old Julian calendar, wassailers would go from orchard to orchard singing and banging drums to frighten away the evil spirits. They would then place pieces of the wassail-soaked toast on the branches of a chosen tree and drink and sing the tree's health in the hope of securing a good crop. This tradition is still carried on in many places in the western counties of England such as Devon, Somerset and Herefordshire, where orchard fruits are predominantly grown, and in Normandy in France.

In the towns, young people would take the wassail bowl around from door to door, and in return for money, food or a small gift they would drink the health of the occupants to the accompaniment of some hearty wassailing songs, such as:

Here we come a-wassailing
Among the leaves so green,
Here we come a-wassailing,
So fair to be seen:
Love and joy come to you,
And to you your wassail too,
And God bless you and send you,
A happy New Year,
And God send you,
A happy New Year

Over time, as Christianity spread and adapted the ancient customs into Christian practice, these wassailing songs became carols, wassailing became carol singing, and New Year became Christmas Eve.

An example of a carol based on a wassailing song is 'We Wish You a Merry Christmas', which was adapted in 1935 by Arthur Warrell from a traditional West Country song. In the lyrics, the singers are demanding some figgy pudding in return for wishing their audience a merry Christmas…

We wish you a merry Christmas,
We wish you a merry Christmas,
We wish you a merry Christmas
And a happy New Year.
Good tidings we bring
To you and your kin;
We wish you a merry Christmas
And a happy New Year!

Oh, bring us some figgy pudding,
Oh, bring us some figgy pudding,
Oh, bring us some figgy pudding,
And bring it right here.
Good tidings we bring
To you and your kin;
We wish you a merry Christmas
And a happy New Year!

Apart from wassailing songs, carols have a variety of other origins. The actual word carol comes from the old French *carole*, meaning a dancing song welcoming the coming of spring, and this in turn comes from the Greek *choros*, 'dancing in a circle', and the Latin *choraula*, a choral song. Carols, in the original sense of the word, have therefore been around for a very long time.

The first carols were not Christmas songs at all but pagan folk songs that were sung as people danced around stone circles during the festivals for the winter solstice. Christians then took these pagan songs and their symbolism and rewrote them with Christian words and imagery.

The very first Christian 'Christmas' carol may have been heard in Rome in AD 129 when, it is said, Pope Telesphorus ordained that 'In the Holy Night of the Nativity of our Lord and Saviour, all shall solemnly sing the Angel's Hymn.'

'The Angel's Hymn' is taken to be 'Gloria in Excelsis Deo', that which was sung by the heavenly host to the shepherds abiding in the field after the Angel of the Lord had announced to them the birth of the Son of God. All hymns and services were sung in Latin then and 'Gloria in Excelsis Deo', which means 'Glory to God in the Highest', was a familiar phrase to those early Christians. 'The Angel's Hymn' has come down to us as the chorus of a well-known 19th-century carol called 'Angels We Have Heard on High'. The verses of this carol are an 1862 English translation by James Chadwick, Bishop of Hexham and Newcastle, of an old French carol 'Les Anges Dans Nos Campagnes' ('Angels in our Fields'), which tells the story of the birth of Christ. It was written long ago by an unknown author and is thought to be based on a song sung by shepherds in medieval France. 'Angels We Have Heard on High' is therefore a fusion of an old shepherd song and the words of the very first Christmas carol as sung by monks since the earliest beginnings of Christianity.

Angels we have heard on high
Sweetly singing o'er the plains
And the mountains in reply
Echoing their joyous strains
Gloria in excelsis Deo
Gloria in excelsis Deo

More carols were written by monks and holy men over the next few hundred years but they tended to be rather dour, deeply theological chants, and since they were written in Latin they didn't gain much traction with those outside the Catholic Church. Then in 1223, after a visit to Bethlehem, St Francis of Assisi started to put on Nativity plays using carols to tell the story. Until that point Christ had been seen as a rather austere, judgemental figure. The Christ of St Francis' Nativity plays was far more friendly and accessible, born into poverty and a simple life, a bringer of joy rather than judgement. People flocked to see the Nativity plays and they were soon being staged all over Europe. So that people could understand them, the carols were performed in the local language and in this way became available for ordinary folk to sing along with.

Popular in France and Germany since the 13th century, carols don't seem to have appeared in England until the 15th century, in a book of devotional poems published in 1426 by a Shropshire monk called John Awdlay, who writes:

'I pray you, sirus, boothe moore and lase,
Sing these caroles in Cristemas.'

He then lists 25 carols based on popular folk and wassailing songs. They were communal songs, meant to be sung by everyone together going from door to door or in the pub or at feasts. This sparked a joyful age of exuberant song writing and carol singing, with carols taken from village to village by wandering minstrels, the words changing all the while to suit local audiences until they became, at best, only loosely based on the Christmas story.

Carols were further encouraged by the Protestant reformer Martin Luther, who championed the use of music in worship and, indeed, wrote new carols himself.

In Britain it all came to a grinding halt when Oliver Cromwell and
his Puritans came to power in 1645. Carols, along with Christmas
itself, were banned from 1649 to 1660, and although they returned
with Charles II at the Restoration, the art of carolling had rather
been lost and Christmas settled into being a subdued affair,
observed privately within the home. And by breaking up the
rural communities where carol singing had thrived, the Industrial
Revolution of the 18th century further hampered the revival of
lusty musical cheer at Christmas.

During this time, however, carols and carol singing were partly
kept alive by the 'waits', bands of men whose official duty was
originally to patrol the streets of towns and cities at night using
musical instruments to warn of any danger. Eventually they
became simply musicians, akin to a town band, and their role was
to welcome distinguished visitors to the town and lead processions.
Waits were abolished in 1835, but at Christmas-time groups of
accomplished singers and musicians known as Christmas waits
would make their way around the town singing carols in return
for money.

The 19th century saw the start of a golden age for carols, sparked
by the publication of a number of collections of ancient carols
by enthusiastic musical historians. The first such collection was
compiled by Davies Gilbert, MP for Bodmin, who sought to
rediscover and preserve the Cornish carols he remembered from
his childhood. His pithily titled volume *Some Ancient Christmas Carols,
With the Tunes to Which They Were Formerly Sung in the West of England*,
published in 1822, with a second edition in 1823, set the ball
rolling. Among the twenty carols included were 'The First Nowell',
'While Shepherds Watched Their Flocks By Night' and 'Christians,
Awake!'. As the British Museum, quoted by Gilbert's publisher
John Nichols, said,

'Mr Gilbert has taken advantage of
old Time, and made safe, for some
centuries at least, a record of our
ancient Christmas Carols; and for this
good deed has secured the gratitude of
Antiquaries yet unborn. These Carols
are genuine national curiosities.'

Next up was William Sandys, a solicitor, who in 1833 brought out a collection of carols called *Christmas Carols Ancient and Modern* which included classics such as 'Mary Mother Meek and Mild', 'A Child this Day is Born' and 'I Saw Three Ships'.

Charles Dickens chose another carol from Sandys' collection to set the scene for his own *Christmas Carol* and give us an indication of the character of the miserly Scrooge: ' ... at the first sound of "God bless you merry, gentlemen, May nothing you dismay!" Scrooge seized the ruler with such energy of action that the singer fled in terror ...'

In 1853 two Anglican vicars, Thomas Helmore and John Neale, came across a 16th-century Finnish manuscript of Latin carols called *Piae Cantiones*, which was full of wonderful tunes that we still sing today such as 'In Dulci Jubilo', 'Good Christian Men Rejoice' and 'Good King Wenceslas'. The two clergymen translated the texts into English and then re-arranged the music for their book *Carols of Christmas-tide*, which came out in 1853.

These books and others such as *Carols, New and Old* by Henry Bramley and John Stainer, published in 1871, all helped lead to a resurgence of interest in carols and also encouraged composers to write new carols as well as modernising older ones, with the result that many of our favourite carols have new words put to old tunes or old words put to new tunes.

Until the latter half of the 19th century the singing of carols took place outside of church services, as many of the songs were considered too racy and irreligious. This changed as the Victorian composers began to compose carols suitable for singing in church as well as adapting older carols for church use.

The first formal church carol service, a Christmas Eve service with Nine Lessons and Carols, was instigated by Edward Benson, Bishop of Truro, in 1880, some say as a way of keeping people out of the pubs. It was actually the suggestion of George Walpole, a member of the cathedral staff who went on to be Bishop of Edinburgh. Benson's son Arthur remembers: 'My father arranged from ancient sources a little service for Christmas Eve – nine carols and nine tiny lessons, which were read by various officers of the Church, beginning with a chorister, and ending, through the different grades, with the Bishop.' The service was held in a wooden structure employed as a temporary cathedral while Truro Cathedral was being built. It was attended by some 400 people and was a great success, setting the template for Christmas Eve carol services everywhere.

Carol services are not confined to Christmas Eve but take place throughout December in the weeks leading up to Christmas. They are often held by candlelight, recalling the days in Victorian times when churches had no electricity and as a way of marking the approaching birth of Christ, the Light of the World.

Carols Around the World

Australia, New Zealand and South Africa

Australia in particular picked up the idea of the candlelight service, and the country's first such service, Carols by Candlelight, was inaugurated in Melbourne in 1937. It has since become a traditional part of the Australian Christmas and takes place in cities across the country during December. The Melbourne event remains Australia's premiere candlelight carol service and is always held on Christmas Eve at the Sydney Myer Music Bowl in the city's King's Domain Gardens, with the singing of traditional carols led by international celebrities and an orchestra. Broadcast on radio since 1937 and on television since 1969, it is now shown on television across New Zealand, much of eastern Asia and many of the Pacific islands.

USA

Almost all the old traditional carols are sung in the United States, having been imported by various waves of immigrants over the years, but there are some well-known home-grown carols as well. Here are three American favourites.

Away in a manger no crib for a bed
The little Lord Jesus laid down his sweet head
The stars in the bright sky looked down where he lay
The little Lord Jesus asleep on the hay

Cracker Joke
How did Mary and
Joseph know how
much baby Jesus
weighed when he
was born?
—
They had a weigh
in a manger!

The words to 'Away in a Manger' first appeared in the Children's
Corner section of an American journal called *The Christian
Cynosure* in March 1882. They were put to music in 1887 by
American composer James R. Murray who claimed they had
been penned by the Protestant reformer Martin Luther himself.
This is almost certainly not true, as the carol was unknown in
Germany until introduced there from America. What is more
likely is that the words came from a songbook put together by
German Lutheran immigrants living in Pennsylvania, thus
making 'Away in a Manger' a genuine American carol. In
England, the carol is sung to a tune written in 1895 by another
American composer, William J. Kirkpatrick.

O little town of Bethlehem

How still we see thee lie

Above thy deep and dreamless sleep

The silent stars go by

The words to 'O Little Town of Bethlehem' were written in 1868
by Phillips Brooks, rector of the Church of the Holy Trinity
in Philadelphia, as a Christmas poem for his Sunday School
children, and were inspired by a visit he had made to Bethlehem
three years earlier. The music was written by his church organist
Louis Redner. A local bookstore owner asked if he could print the
song on a leaflet for sale and this was seen by Dr William Reed
Huntingdon, rector of a church in Massachusetts, who published
it in his hymnal for Sunday schools, The Church Porch. It
became an instant success in America and was introduced into
England by the composer Ralph Vaughan Williams in 1906. He
wrote a new arrangement for it based on an English folk tune
called The Ploughboy's Dream which he had learned from a
labourer of Forest Green, a village near his home in Surrey.

Not exactly a carol but a hugely popular American Christmas song, 'Jingle Bells' was actually written for Thanksgiving by the composer and songwriter James Lord Pierpoint, uncle of the financier J. P. Morgan. It was first printed and performed (by minstrels) in Boston in 1857 under the title 'One Horse Open Sleigh', but after one of Pierpoint's friends described the song as a 'merry little jingle' it was reissued as 'Jingle Bells'. It is not clear where he actually wrote the song, but it was said to have been inspired by the sleigh races in the town of Medford in Massachusetts, and there is a plaque in the town centre on the site of the former Simpson Tavern that claims Pierpoint wrote 'Jingle Bells' there in 1850. Not a lot of people know that 'Jingle Bells' was the first song ever broadcast from space. Just before Christmas in 1965 the astronauts on Gemini VI played it on a harmonica and sleigh bells to accompany a spoof report of seeing Santa Claus fly by in his sleigh.

Jingle bells
Jingle bells
Jingle all the way
Oh what fun it is to ride
In a one-horse open sleigh

Canada

The first carol of the New World was written in around 1642 by a French Jesuit priest called Jean de Bréheuf, who went to North America as a missionary to work among the Huron Indians living in the Great Lakes area. The carol, which was set to the tune of an old French folk song, was written in the Huron language and called 'Jesous Ahatohnia' ('Jesus is Born'). Jean de Bréheuf, later St Jean, was killed when the Huron mission was destroyed by the Iroquois Indians in 1649, but his carol lived on and is now celebrated as a Canadian national treasure, appearing in Anglican hymn books and on several albums by well-known singers such as Burl Ives, Bruce Cockburn and Tom Jackson.

France

While shepherds watched

Their flocks by night

All seated on the ground

The angel of the Lord came down

And glory shone around

Many of the most ancient carols come from France, one notable example being 'Angels We Have Heard on High', which was adapted from the old French shepherd song 'Les Anges Dans Nos Campagnes' ('Angels in our Fields' – see page 72). It is entirely possible that England's Poet Laureate Nahum Tate based his carol, the schoolchildren's favourite, 'While Shepherds Washed Their Socks', sorry, 'While Shepherds Watched Their Flocks by Night' on 'Les Anges Dans Nos Campagnes'. Both songs describe the story of the angels announcing the birth of Christ to the shepherds in the field, from Chapter 2 of St Luke's Gospel in the Bible, and it is not too much of a stretch to think that Tate might have come across the old French song on his travels. (Interestingly, in St Luke's Gospel it refers to shepherds in the field, singular, keeping watch over the flock, singular).

'While Shepherds Watched Their Flocks by Night' first appeared in 1700 in *A Supplement to the New Version of the Psalms* by Dr Brady and Mr Tate and, because of its religious content and inclusion with the Psalms, was the only carol that was allowed to be used in church services during the whole of the 18th century. In England it is most commonly set to a tune called Winchester Old, an arrangement of a melody by the 16th-century composer Christopher Tye.

Germany

O Christmas tree, O Christmas tree,
Your branches green delight us!
They are green when summer days are bright,
They are green when winter snow is white.
O Christmas tree, O Christmas tree,
Your branches green delight us!

As with France, many English carols come from traditional German folk songs and shepherd songs (*Hirtenlieder*). Perhaps the one we know best is Germany's favourite carol 'O Tannenbaum' ('O Christmas Tree'), which was originally a 16th-century folk song written as an ode to the fir tree's lasting evergreen qualities. For centuries in Germany the fir tree had been firmly associated with Christmas, and in 1824 a composer from Leipzig called Ernst Anschutz added some verses that turned the fir tree into a Christmas tree and 'O Tannenbaum' became a carol. The man who is said to have first brought a fir tree inside for Christmas, Martin Luther, was also a prolific writer of carols, many of which are still sung in Germany today.

Austria

Silent night, holy night,
All is calm, all is bright
Round yon virgin mother and child.
Holy infant, so tender and mild,
Sleep in heavenly peace,
Sleep in heavenly peace.

Austria is the home of one of the most famous and beloved carols of them all, 'Silent Night'. This is another carol that could have been inspired by the old French shepherd song 'Les Anges Dans Nos Campagnes' for it, too, tells the tale of the angel appearing to the shepherds in the fields from the Gospel of St Luke. There is a romantic tale of how this romantic carol came to be written which may or may not be true, but I want it to be true so here goes. The words were written in 1816 by a young Catholic priest called Josef Mohr (1792–1848) as he sat in the mountains above his home village of Mariapfarr in Austria gazing down at the peaceful snowy scene below. Two years later, he was due to take midnight mass in the little church of Oberndorf near Salzburg but found that mice had chewed through the church organ and there was nothing to play music on. So Josef went to see his friend in the next village, schoolmaster and organist Franz Gruber, and asked him to compose a tune for his poem that could be played on the guitar. Gruber did just that and 'Silent Night' was sung for the first time at midnight mass in Oberndorf in 1818 with Gruber accompanying on the guitar. When the organ mender Karl Mauracher came to repair the organ after Christmas, Gruber tested out the instrument by playing 'Silent Night', and Karl was so taken with it that he took a copy to give to his friends the Strassers, a well-known family of travelling singers, who put it into their Christmas repertoire. They sang it for Frederick William IV of Prussia, who so loved it he ordered that 'Silent Night' should be sung by his cathedral choir every Christmas Eve. The original manuscript was lost and for a time it was thought that 'Silent Night' was the work of a famous composer such as Mozart, Beethoven or Haydn, but in 1995 a manuscript in Mohr's handwriting and dated 1820 was discovered, proving that Mohr wrote the words and Gruber the music.

The carol was first translated into English for a Methodist Episcopal Church in New York by J. F. Warner in 1849, then in 1858 by hymn writer Emily Elliott for the choir of St Mark's Church, Brighton, in England. The definitive version we know and sing today was translated by John Freeman Young, an American clergyman in New York, in 1859.

'Silent Night' has gone on to become one of the most famous carols ever written and has been translated into over a hundred languages. The version sung by Bing Crosby in 1935 has sold 30 million copies and is the third best selling single of all time. 'Silent Night' has been voted Britain's favourite carol more times than any other carol.

Another, even older carol that became a Christmas favourite and even made it into the Christmas pop charts, was the 14th-century melody 'In Dulci Jubilo' ('In Sweet Rejoicing'), which reached No 4 in 1975 with an instrumental version by Mike Oldfield.

The World's Favourite Christmas Songs

Since we are talking about the music charts, maybe we should take a quick look at some popular Christmas songs that are not necessarily religious but have a Christmas theme. Several of the best-selling songs of all time have Christmas themes and, in chart terms, the US and UK Christmas No 1 spot has always been the most sought after No 1 spot of the year. A good Christmas song may only sell at Christmas-time but it will sell at every Christmas-time, year after year after year.

Here are some of the songs that have become as much a part of Christmas as 'Once in Royal David's City' and 'Hark the Herald Angels Sing'.

White Christmas

'White Christmas' is the best-selling song of all time. It was written by Irving Berlin in 1940 as a Christmas song for Bing Crosby to sing in the 1942 film *Holiday Inn*. Berlin actually wrote the words while sunning himself by the pool at a Beverley Hills hotel, but got his inspiration by recalling the Christmases he used to know in his home town of New York. He wrote the music overnight and when he had finished he is said to have proclaimed, 'This is the best song I ever wrote – heck, this is the best song anybody ever wrote!' He was not wrong. Bing Crosby's recording of the song for Decca sold over 50 million copies, the biggest seller of Crosby's career. In all, including covers and albums, 'White Christmas' has sold well over 100 million copies. It has been recorded by numerous diverse artists such as Doris Day, the Beach Boys, Bob Marley and Bob Dylan. The *Holiday Inn* version won the Oscar for Best Original Song in 1943. The song spawned its own musical film, *White Christmas*, the highest grossing film of 1954. And its success proved that a secular song could become as much a part of Christmas as a carol – in fact, 'White Christmas' has become a Christmas hymn.

Rudolph the Red-Nosed Reindeer

This began life as a story written by a young advertising copywriter called Robert Lewis May in 1939. May was asked by his employers, the department store Montgomery Ward, to write a story for a Christmas colouring book to give away to children as a promotional tool. May came up with the tale of a reindeer who is teased and excluded because of his bright red nose, but becomes a hero when he guides Santa's sleigh through a foggy Christmas Eve by the light of his nose. Montgomery Ward were nervous at first because of the association of red noses with drunkenness, but they went ahead anyway and ended up giving away two and a half million copies of the book in that 1939 Christmas season alone, and continued handing out millions of copies every year until paper shortages caused by the Second World War put a stop to it. In 1948, May persuaded his brother-in-law, Johnny Marks, to put the story to music and the resulting song was used to accompany a Rudolph cartoon released in cinemas in 1948. At first May was unable to find an artist to record the song as a single but eventually, in 1949, Gene Autry, the 'Singing Cowboy', reluctantly recorded it as a 'B' side to appease his wife, who loved it, so we are told. The Gene Autry single sold 1.75 million copies in its first Christmas season and since then, in all versions, it has racked up well over 100 million sales, making it the second best selling song of all time after 'White Christmas'. 'Rudolph the Red-Nosed Reindeer' really has gone down in history.

Cracker Joke
What did Rudolph say before telling his latest joke?

—

'This one'll sleigh you'

The Christmas Song — Chestnuts Roasting on an Open Fire

Written by Bob Wells and Mel Tormé in 1945, Wells began writing lyrics about winter as a way of mentally keeping cool during a hot summer in California's San Fernando Valley. His writing partner, the singer and composer Mel Tormé, dropped by and saw some ideas jotted down on a pad: chestnuts, Jack Frost, Yuletide, Eskimos …

'I think you've got a song here', he said, sitting down at the piano, and in 30 minutes they wrote what would become the most performed song of all time. Their music publisher was not impressed, claiming that the song was all about Christmas Eve and that no one would buy a song that could only be played on one day of the year. Humbug. When Wells and Tormé took it to their friend Nat King Cole he listened to it once and then leaped out of his chair and said, very firmly, 'Nobody gets that song but me …' It became Nat King Cole's biggest hit.

Other Christmas favourites

Another standard without which no Christmas, and certainly
no American Christmas, would be complete is 'Winter
Wonderland', written in 1934, with music by Felix Bernard and
words by Richard Smith. Smith was inspired to write the lyrics
by children playing in a snow-covered park outside the window
of his sanatorium in Pennsylvania where he was recovering
from tuberculosis. It has been recorded by more top artists than
almost any other record, including Perry Como, Frank Sinatra,
Johnny Mathis, Dean Martin, Ella Fitzgerald, Lena Horne,
Tony Bennett, Elvis Presley, The Carpenters, Eurythmics, Neil
Diamond, Barry Manilow, Dolly Parton, Bing Crosby ...

Then there's 'Santa Claus is Comin' to Town', written in 1934 by
John Coots and Haven Gillespie and recorded by the likes of Bing
Crosby, Bruce Springsteen, The Crystals, Mariah Carey and the
Jackson 5, and, of course, 'I'll be Home for Christmas', written by
Kim Gannon and Walter Kent for American soldiers overseas
during the Second World War and recorded by Bing Crosby in
1943.

If all you want for Christmas is world domination, Bing Crosby,
it would seem, is the key, although there are a few songs that have
wheedled their way into the Christmas season without him: 'Do
They Know It's Christmas' by Band Aid, 'Mary's Boy Child'
by Harry Belafonte and again by Boney M, 'Last Christmas'
by Wham, 'When a Child is Born' by Johnny Mathis, 'I Wish
it Could Be Christmas Every Day' by Wizzard, 'Wonderful
Christmas Time' by Paul McCartney or even, perhaps, if one is
feeling especially mellow, Cliff Richard's 'Mistletoe and Wine'.

Britain's top Christmas No 1 is 'Do They Know It's Christmas'
by Band Aid, which sold a record 3.69 million copies when it first
came out in 1984. The song became the Christmas No 1 two
more times, for Band Aid II in 1989 and for Band Aid 20 in 2004
and went on to sell nearly 12 million copies altogether, becoming
the second biggest selling UK record of all time after Elton John's
1997 tribute to Princess Diana 'Candle in the Wind'.

The Beatles are the only group to have reached No 1 at Christmas four times, the first three times consecutively from 1963 to 1965 with 'I Want to Hold Your Hand', 'I Feel Fine', and 'Day Tripper' and again in 1967 with 'Hello, Goodbye'.

The Spice Girls also achieved three consecutive Christmas No 1s from 1996 to 1998 with '2 Become 1', 'Too Much' and 'Goodbye'.

Paul McCartney has been at No 1 for Christmas more times than any other artist, four times with the Beatles, once with Wings in 1977 with 'Mull of Kintyre', the first UK record to sell over 2 million copies, once with Band Aid in 1984, again with Band Aid 20 in 2004 and finally in 2012 with The Justice Collective and 'He Ain't Heavy, He's My Brother'. Cliff Richard and Spice Girl Mel C are the next most successful Christmas artists, having both achieved four Christmas No 1s with various acts.

'Bohemian Rhapsody' by Queen is the only song to reach No 1 at Christmas twice with the same artist, in 1975 and again in 1991, after Freddie Mercury's death, while 'Mary's Boy Child' became Christmas No 1 twice with different artists, Harry Belafonte in 1957 and Boney M in 1978. 'Last Christmas' by Wham! was destined for the Christmas No 1 spot in 1984 but missed out to Band Aid, although this meant that George Michael was at both No 1 and No 2, and 'Last Christmas' became the best selling Christmas No 2 of all time.

The rock band Slade are said to be the highest Christmas earners, receiving some £500,000 every year from sales of their 1973 Christmas No 1 'Merry Xmas Everybody'.

It makes you feel all Christmassy just reading about them – which is very appropriate as we have finally reached Christmas …

Cracker Joke
What do you call two chess players showing off about their intellectual prowess in a hotel lobby?

—

Chess nuts boasting in an open foyer!

In the UK, the Twelve Days of Christmas begin at sunset on Christmas Eve, 24 December, and finish on Epiphany Eve, the evening of 5 January, commonly known as Twelfth Night.

The Twelve Days have long been celebrated by the Church as a run of feast days linking Christmas and the birth of Christ with Epiphany, which celebrates the baptism of Christ by John the Baptist.

The concept of a twelve-day festival echoes the pagan festivals of the Druids and of the Norse Yule, during which a (Yule) log was collected on the day of the winter solstice, doused in ale or cider, decorated with evergreens, set alight and then allowed to smoulder for twelve days before being ceremoniously extinguished.

When it comes to the Twelve Days of Christmas we can see that the secular and religious Christmas 'seasons' are complete opposites. The secular Christmas season begins with 'Advent' in late November and encompasses all the activities we have been talking about: Christmas cards, carols, Christmas markets and shopping, Christmas trees and decorations. The build-up then comes to a climax with a huge meal and the opening of presents on Christmas Day and sort of peters out in a hangover on Boxing Day. The religious Christmas season, on the other hand, begins on Christmas Day and then continues for twelve days of celebration for the birth of Christ, culminating in his baptism and introduction to the world on Epiphany, 6 January. Advent, for the Church, is merely the period of waiting anxiously for the arrival of Christ.

A quick word here about the Eastern and Western churches, because we are mainly concerned in this book with Christmas as celebrated in the English-speaking nations and Western European countries whose major influence has been the Western Church.

In the 4th century, Christianity became the official religion of the Roman Empire. In the 5th century, the Western Roman Empire collapsed, while the Eastern Roman Empire was reorganised with Constantinople as its capital and Greek as its official language. During all this the churches of the Eastern and Western Roman Empires diverged as well, into Greek-influenced Orthodox in the East and Latin-influenced Roman Catholic, and later Protestant, in the West. The Churches adopted different liturgies and festivals and were also shaped by different Western and Oriental cultures and traditions. This is a huge simplification of a complex history and the two Churches have much in common, but it does help to explain why the Western Church and the Eastern Church do things a bit differently at Christmas.

The Twelve Days of Christmas were first mentioned in the 4th century by a doctor of the Eastern Orthodox Church called Ephrem the Syriac, who described them as a continuous 'festal tide'. This was confirmed at the second Council of Tours in AD 567. There were a number of councils held in the French city of Tours between AD 461 and 1153 at which church leaders would get together to decide on church protocols, and during the second council in AD 567 they agreed to combine the Christmas of the Western Church with the Epiphany of the Eastern Church by observing the feast days of various saints on each of the twelve days in between.

In the Laws of King Ethelred, who reigned in England between 978 and 1016, the Twelve Days of Christmas are ordained to be 'a time of peace and concord among Christian men, when all strife must cease'. A time of good will to all men, no less.

In the Middle Ages, and in Tudor times, the religious fundamentals of the Twelve Days were rather lost among the more pagan elements of unrestrained feasting and roistering, which is one of the reasons why the Puritans banned Christmas.

Today the religious connotations of the Twelve Days are still rather glossed over although Christmas Eve and Christmas Day still have resonance. Boxing Day and New Year have a more secular significance and Twelfth Night is when people traditionally take down the Christmas tree and Christmas decorations.

The idea of the Twelve Days of Christmas is perhaps best kept alive for us today in one of our most beloved Christmas Carols called, spookily enough, 'The Twelve Days of Christmas'.

On the twelfth day of Christmas
My true love sent to me:
Twelve Drummers Drumming
Eleven Pipers Piping
Ten Lords a Leaping
Nine Ladies Dancing
Eight Maids a Milking
Seven Swans a Swimming
Six Geese a Laying
Five Gold Rings
Four Calling Birds
Three French Hens
Two Turtle Doves
and a Partridge in a Pear Tree

The words of the song first appeared in print as a poem, without music, in a children's book called *Mirth Without Mischief*, published in 1780. The book outlines 'Twelve Pleasing Pastimes' from Britain's past, and since this was a book about games it seems reasonable to assume that the poem began life as a cumulative verse game of 'memory and forfeit', a sort of verbal musical chairs, played during the Twelfth Night festivities. Everyone would gather round in a circle and then a chosen master of ceremonies would start off with the first verse, 'On the first day of Christmas my true love sent to me – a partridge in a pear tree.' Each member of the company would then recite the first verse in turn. The master of ceremonies would then add the second verse about turtle doves and each person would recite the first and second verses in turn. Then the third would be added and each would recite all three verses and so on. And as the game progressed the verses would be spoken a little faster. Each time someone forgot a line or made a mistake they would forfeit their place in the game. The winner would be the first person to correctly recite all twelve verses at speed. Not easy after a glass or two of Christmas cheer or if your mouth is all gummed up with Christmas toffee.

Decoding the Song

The words of the song are thought to have come from a 16th-century English translation of an old French song. This would go some way to explaining the partridge in a pear tree. An English partridge, you see, would never be seen perching in a pear tree, whereas the French red-legged partridge is never happier than when nestling among its leaves. And the French word for partridge is *perdrix*, pronounced 'peardree' and so it is easy to see how in translation, in the context of partridges, a perdrix might become a pear tree.

Although there are many theories as to what all the various gifts mean, it seems likely that they are all features of the feasting and partying of the Twelve Days of Christmas in the Middle Ages, both in France and England – ingredients from the table, lords and ladies leaping and dancing, pipers and drummers playing.

The words of 'The Twelve Days of Christmas' were occasionally put to music in the 19th century but the definitive setting was written in 1909 by Frederic Austin, who adapted a traditional folk song melody and re-ordered some of the lyrics. He also instituted the drawn-out flourishing of 'five gold rings', giving everyone a chance to show off their vocal prowess.

Now let's take a look at the three of the Twelve Days of Christmas we still celebrate fully: Christmas Eve, Christmas Day and Boxing Day.

Cracker Joke
Knock knock!
Who's there?
Hanna
Hanna who?
—
Hanna partridge
in a pear tree!

We tend to think of the whole day of 24 December as Christmas Eve but, technically, Christmas Eve doesn't begin until sunset on that day. This is because, in the Christian calendar, night comes before day, a belief drawn from the Book of Genesis, Chapter 1, verse 5, describing the Creation of the world: 'And God called the light Day, and the darkness he called Night. And there was evening and there was morning, one day.'

For this reason 24 December is not a public holiday, at least in Britain and North America, although some countries in South America, Scandinavia and Eastern European do treat it as a holiday or at least as an early closing day.

Cracker Joke
What did Adam say to his wife on the day before Christmas?

—

'It's Christmas, Eve!'

Festival of Nine Lessons and Carols from King's College, Cambridge

For many people, not just in Britain but around the world, Christmas undoubtedly begins at 3 p.m. on Christmas Eve with the most famous carol service in the world, the Festival of Nine Lessons and Carols from King's College, Cambridge. King's College chapel is often described as 'the most beautiful building in the world', the choir of King's as 'the best choir in the world' and Festival of Nine Lessons and Carols the 'loveliest carol service in the world'. It was instigated in 1918, at the close of World War One by the Dean of King's, Eric Milner-White, an ex-army chaplain, as a way of making Church of England services more dynamic and accessible. The Order of Service was adapted from a service devised and presided over by future Archbishop of Canterbury, Edward Benson, in 1880 when he was the Bishop of Truro.

In 1919, the order of the lessons in the King's College service was revised slightly and one of its most cherished features was introduced: the singing of the first verse of the carol 'Once in Royal David's City' by a solo boy chorister to open the proceedings. The chorister chosen to sing the solo is not told until the last minute so that he doesn't get too nervous beforehand, and as he will be performing unaccompanied in front of millions of people all over the world this is probably wise – I can tell you from experience that there are a couple of high notes at the end that can ambush the finest of choristers ...

'Once in Royal David's City', one of our most popular carols, was written by Cecil Frances Alexander, wife of the future Bishop of Derry, for her hymn book *Hymns for Little Children*, published in 1848, and was set to music in 1849 by the English organist Henry Gauntlett. Cecil Frances Alexander was one of the most popular hymn writers of the Victorian era. She wrote over 400 hymns, including 'All Things Bright and Beautiful' and 'There Is a Green Hill Far Away'.

As well as traditionally beginning with 'Once in Royal David's City', the King's College Festival of Nine Lessons and Carols traditionally ends with 'Hark! the Herald Angels Sing', a carol that has attained glorious perfection *despite* its original composers rather than by virtue of them. The words were written in 1739 by England's most prolific hymn writer, composer of some 6,000 hymns, the Methodist co-founder Charles Wesley. The work was intended as a 'Hymn for Christmas Day' for his brother John Wesley's collection Hymns and Sacred Poems. Wesley's opening lines were 'Hark! how all the Welkin rings, Glory to the King of Kings', but these were changed to the now familiar 'Hark! the Herald Angels Sing, Glory to the new-born King!' by Wesley's Methodist colleague George Whitefield, much to Wesley's annoyance. He didn't mind people reprinting his hymns, he once wrote, provided they printed them as they were written and did not 'attempt to mend them ...'

As for the music ... well, Wesley was rather a gloomy fellow who preferred his words set to slow, solemn music and he would have been just as horrified by the up-tempo tune we sing out to today as he was by the meddling with his words. In 1840, over one hundred years after Wesley wrote his hymn, the German composer Felix Mendelssohn composed a cantata to celebrate the 400th anniversary of the Gutenberg printing press, and in 1855 an English musician called William Cummings took the piece and adapted it to fit the words of 'Hark! the Herald Angels Sing'. Mendelssohn was dead by then, perhaps fortunately, for he would have been just as incensed as Wesley, having decreed that his music would 'never work with sacred tunes'. So 'Hark! the Herald Angels Sing', one of the most beautiful and beloved carols of them all, was cobbled together with words the writer didn't write and music the composer thought thoroughly unsuitable for a carol.

The King's College service has been broadcast on BBC radio annually since 1928 (except, for some unknown reason, in 1930) and has become a much-loved part of the British Christmas Eve.

In order to attend the King's College Festival of Nine Lessons and Carols, members of the general public have to queue up outside the chapel from early on the morning of Christmas Eve. There is, however, another popular Christmas Eve service that requires no such privations – midnight mass.

Midnight Mass

It is generally agreed that Jesus must have been born at night, as we are told in the Gospel of St Luke that the shepherds were watching their flock by night when the angel informed them of his birth. Hence the mass that celebrates the birth of Jesus is held at midnight or shortly before and includes a candlelit vigil to represent the coming of the Light of the World. A particular belief that some hold is that on the stroke of midnight all sheep in the fields turn to the East and kneel.

The first midnight mass was held in the Basilica of St Maria Maggiore in Rome in AD 432 at the behest of Pope Sixtus III. He got the idea from the writings of a Christian woman called Egeria who, in AD 380, had made a pilgrimage to Jerusalem and witnessed the midnight vigil observed on Christmas Eve by Christians there. Sixtus had an underground chapel built to replicate the cave in Bethlehem where Jesus is thought to have been born (now under the Church of the Nativity in Bethlehem), and it was in this chapel that the first midnight mass took place.

Midnight mass is attended by Catholics and Protestants alike, while Eastern churches hold a midnight vigil rather than a mass.

Customs and traditions associated with Christmas Eve vary around the world. In Eastern European countries such as Lithuania, Poland, Ukraine, the Czech Republic and Slovakia, the main Christmas meal is eaten on Christmas Eve, and because Christmas Eve is the last day of the Advent fast in the East, the main dish is fish; no meat is allowed.

There is no doubt that Christmas Eve is, if not the spookiest night of the year (that would be Halloween), then certainly the most magical. To begin with, there are many superstitions that persist from the pagan times about this night, the longest and darkest night of the year. Animals can speak. Water turns to wine. Lost treasures are revealed. Some think the dead revisit their earthly homes. Ghostly figures move in the night.

The most welcome figure moving in the night on Christmas Eve is, of course, Father Christmas. Or Santa Claus.

So who is Father Christmas? Or Santa Claus?

'The personification of Christmas as
a benevolent old man with a flowing
white beard, wearing a red sleeved gown
and hood trimmed with white fur, and
carrying a sack of Christmas presents.'

Oxford English Dictionary

Father Christmas as we know him today is an amalgam of
many different characters, real and imagined, but there are
two figures in particular who can be considered his closest
ancestors. These two are the English Father Christmas, whose
roots go right back to pagan harbingers of spring, and Santa
Claus, a Dutch American figure loosely based on St Nicholas,
a 4th-century Bishop of Myra in what is now Turkey.

The English Father Christmas

The English Father Christmas has evolved over many centuries. In pagan prehistoric Britain, a common feature of the many different winter festivals was the appearance of a figure dressed in green and wreathed in evergreen plants such as holly, ivy and mistletoe, representing hope and the coming of spring. Although we know little about such figures, the idea of a 'Green Man' who embodies the spirit of rebirth and fertility is ever present in folklore. Somewhat bizarrely, considering that he is a heathen figure, the 'Green Man' figure lives on in numerous church sculptures and carvings, where he is depicted as a face mingled with leaves, vines and flowers.

The equivalent figure in Roman Britain was Saturn, god of sowing and seed, who was celebrated during the midwinter festival of Saturnalia.

When the Saxons invaded and settled in England in the 5th and 6th centuries they introduced their own custom of personifying the various elements of nature with characters such as Father Time, Father Frost or Father Snow. In December, in the middle of the winter, someone from the community would be chosen to play the part of Father Winter. Clad in green robes edged with white fur to represent ice and snow, he would be welcomed into people's homes, where he was invited to sit by the fire and plied with food and drink in the hope that such hospitality would be repaid with a mild winter. Could this be why some folk today leave out a mince pie and a tot of whisky or sherry for Father Christmas on Christmas Eve? And with all those mince pies, no wonder Father Christmas has become a tad rotund.

Next came the Vikings, who brought with them Odin, a Norse god of many characters. For twelve days at the end of December, Odin would visit the Earth in the guise of one of those characters, a chap named Jul, from whom we get the term Yule. During Yuletide, Jul, a plump, elderly, white-bearded fellow in a long, blue, hooded cloak, travelled around the world on an eight-legged horse called Sleipnir, handing out gifts from his sack to those who had been good, and dishing out punishment to those who had been bad. The similarities to Father Christmas are unmistakable. Plump. White beard. Hooded cloak. A sack full of presents. And he could travel all around the world in a very short time. Alright, Jul had an eight-legged horse rather than eight reindeer, but close enough. And, as the song tells us, 'He knows if you've been bad or good, So be good for goodness sake!'

So, by the time we reach the 11th century, the idea of a jolly Christmas figure had become pretty well established in England. The second phase in the development of the modern Father Christmas begins with the Norman Conquest in 1066. But first we need to go back a bit in history to the Europe of the 3rd century AD, and the birth of a fellow called Nicholas.

St Nicholas of Myra

Nicholas was born to wealthy Greek parents in about AD 270 in Patara, a small port on the Mediterranean Sea near Myra, in what is now Turkey. His parents died when he was a boy, leaving Nicholas a very wealthy young man, but he was a devout Christian and gave much of his fortune away to the poor and needy.

There are numerous stories of Nicholas' generosity but the most famous one concerns a neighbour of his in Myra, a poor man with three daughters. It was the custom in those days to pay a dowry to the bridegroom when a girl was married (a custom still observed today in some societies), but the poor neighbour had no money to pay a dowry for any of his daughters, and so they were destined to end up unmarried and perhaps sold into slavery or, even worse, sent to work in a house of ill repute. Nicholas was moved to help them and decided to give each girl a bag of gold coins on the eve of her coming of age to use as a dowry. Knowing the family would be too proud to accept charity, Nicholas waited until night fell and flung a bag of gold coins for the eldest daughter in through the open window of the neighbour's house and hurried away. The following year he did the same with a bag of gold for the second daughter. When it came to the third daughter, the girl's father determined to find out who it was that was giving them money, and he lay in wait by the window. Nicholas, however, was wise to this and changed his approach. Instead of throwing the bag in through the open window he climbed on to the roof and dropped it down the chimney, where it landed in a stocking that one of the girls had hung by the chimney to dry.

This is why, of course, we hang up our stockings on Christmas Eve. It is also why we hang chocolate coins wrapped in gold foil on the Christmas tree. And, because he was seen as someone who helped those in financial difficulties, St Nicholas became the patron saint of pawnbrokers. The sign of three gold balls that pawnbrokers hang outside their premises recalls the three bags of gold that Nicholas gave to his neighbour's daughters so that they could marry.

Thanks to this story, and others like it, Nicholas came to be known as a bringer of gifts, and he was later sanctified as the patron saint of children. Now, you may have spotted a flaw in the tale at this point. If no one knew that it was Nicholas who was giving out bags of gold coins, how did he get his reputation for generosity? Well, he performed many other acts of kindness too, and you can't go around committing acts of kindness on such a major scale without somebody noticing, and once his name was out there people came from far and wide to tell their own anecdotes about this reclusive benefactor. St Nicholas became the subject of countless legends and had many miracles attributed to him. He was venerated throughout Europe, including by the Normans who, in 1066, brought the cult of St Nicholas with them to England. Indeed, since St Nicholas was also patron saint of sailors, having reportedly rescued three sailors from a terrible storm at sea, William the Conqueror is said to have prayed to him for a safe crossing of the English Channel before he set sail to invade England. The Normans spread the cult of St Nicholas throughout the country and today there are more than 400 churches dedicated to St Nicholas to be found in England alone.

St Nicholas is thought to have died in AD 343 on 6 December, and so 6 December was made his feast day, a day which was widely celebrated throughout medieval Europe. On St Nicholas' Eve (5 December), more particularly on the Continent, children would put out a shoe or some other receptacle in the hope that they would wake up to find that overnight St Nicholas had filled it with sweets or other goodies.

And so medieval England now had two characters to choose from at Christmas-time. But whereas St Nicholas was seen as a gift giver and a religious personality, the English Christmas figure was more about drinking and merry making, although the first known personification of Christmas in England seems to have been a mix of the two.

He is found in a carol written in the mid 15th century by a rector from Devon called Richard Smart.

Nowell, Nowell, Nowell, Nowell

Who ys ther syngeth so

I am here, syre Christemas,

Welcome my lord syre Christemas

Sir Christmas then goes on to tell of the news of Christ's birth.

God be with you, Sir, tidings I you bring,
A maid hath born a child full young,
The which causeth me to sing.

                              Nowell.

And he finishes by extolling the company to

Drink you all right heartily
Make good cheer and be right merry

The Tudors had no problem with drinking 'right heartily',
making 'good cheer' and being 'right merry'. Indeed, the early
Tudors happily continued a riotous custom from medieval
England where a member from the lower orders of a household
would be appointed as the Lord of Misrule, whose job it was to
take charge of the Christmas revelries and ensure a full degree
of drunkenness and debauchery. In Scotland he was known as
the Abbot of Unreason.

This is how the historian John Stow describes the Lord
of Misrule in his *Survey of London*, published in 1603:

'In the feaste of Christmas, there was
in the kinges house, wheresoeuer hee
was lodged, a Lord of Misrule, or
Maister of merry disports, and the like
had yee in the house of euery noble
man, of honor, or good worshippe,
were he spirituall or temporall.'

The Church had their own version of the Lord of Misrule, the Boy Bishop, a chorister elected on St Nicholas Day to take the place of the Bishop until Holy Innocents Day on 28 December. During this time the Boy Bishop would dress in full bishop's robes, sit on the bishop's throne and perform all the ceremonies in the cathedral except for mass.

Then came the Protestant Reformation in Europe, and by the start of the 17th century there was a whiff of Puritanism in the air. Some in England began to question the excesses of Christmas. St Nicholas, a Catholic saint, was got rid of without much complaint, and the Lord of Misrule died out, but the English Christmas figure was defended by those like James I who saw no problem in Protestants observing traditional Christmas celebrations. In 1616 the playwright Ben Jonson wrote a masque for the royal court of James I called *Christmas his Masque*, in which the Christmas figure protests against his exclusion by the Puritans.

'Why Gentlemen, doe you know what you doe? ha! would you ha'kept me out? Christmas, old Christmas? Christmas of London, and Captaine Christmas?'

In the end, all the jollity and enjoyment became just too much for the Puritans, who not only disapproved of the gluttony and sloth engendered by Christmas but were offended by the very name of Christmas itself, with its implicit reference to the Catholic mass. When Oliver Cromwell came to power in 1645 Christmas was sent packing, and Father Christmas along with it. The ban on Christmas, however, was very unpopular and various Royalist writers and pamphleteers bravely tried to keep the idea of Christmas alive.

In 1658, the year in which Cromwell died, we come across the first ever written reference to 'Father Christmas' in the title of a short book written by Josiah King, *The Examination and Tryall of Old Father Christmas*. In the book an old white-haired Father Christmas is put on trial for charges brought by the Commonwealth,

'... thou art here Indited by the name of Christmas, of the Town of Superstition in the County of Idolatry, and that thou hast from time to time abused the people of this Common-wealth, drawing and inticing them to Drunkennesse, Gluttony, and unlawful Gaming, Wantonnesse, Uncleanness, Lasciviousness, Cursing, Swearing, abuse of the Creatures, some to one Vice, and some to another, all to Idleness ...'

You will be glad to hear that Father Christmas was cleared of all the charges and with the Restoration of Charles II he was once again welcome in England. The outrageous excesses of the medieval and Tudor Christmas celebrations, however, did not come back. Even though the Restoration royal court was famously licentious and dissolute, Christmas itself, as celebrated by what was by then a largely Protestant country, became muted and Father Christmas had somewhat lost his bounce.

Mummers' Plays

His spirit, though, was kept alive in the mummers' plays. These plays, or sometimes mimes, were performed in pubs or in people's houses at Christmas-time. A troupe of local men would go from house to house or from pub to pub to perform, with the aim of raising money.

The plays had their origins in pagan winter ceremonies, with players acting out the triumph of spring over the dark days of winter. They were based on folk tales and always involved a fight between good and evil, with someone being killed and then brought back to life. A popular Christianised plotline was the legend of St George and the Dragon, featuring a gallant Christian St George figure being slain by an evil Turkish knight and then getting restored to life by a comic doctor – a parable of death and rebirth. Full of bawdy characters such as a fool dressed in a cap and bells and men in women's clothing, mummers' plays became very popular in the 18th century and were often presented by a subversive Christmas figure issuing a rebuke to the party-poopers: 'In comes I, Old Father Christmas, Be I welcome or be I not, I hope that Christmas will ne'er be forgot.'

Our modern-day pantomime or 'panto' has its roots in the mummers' plays, which contained all the stock elements so beloved in panto: the stage fights, the slapstick humour, the double entendres, the role reversal and cross-dressing characters, the comic dame, the audience participation ('Boo, hiss … He's behind you!') and the triumph of good over evil.

It was the Victorians, however, in their quest to bring back the old Christmas spirit of the past, who finally rescued Father Christmas from the doldrums and established him once more in his rightful place at the centre of the Christmas celebrations. They took elements from all the previous Christmas figures and came up with a cheery, chuckling, gent with a thick beard and a long, hooded tunic, which could be green, red or blue. The definitive Victorian Father Christmas is the Ghost of Christmas Present as described by Charles Dickens in *A Christmas Carol*, published in 1843. He possesses many of the traditional characteristics, and even wears a pagan holly wreath.

'I am the Ghost of Christmas Present,' said the Spirit. 'Look upon me.' Scrooge reverently did so. It was clothed in one simple green robe, or mantle, bordered with white fur … and on its head it wore no other covering than a holly wreath, set here and there with shining icicles. Its dark brown curls were long and free; free as its genial face, its sparkling eye, its open hand, its cheery voice, its unconstrained demeanor, and its joyful air.'

The Father Christmas we know and love is taking shape. But, he has a rival.

Cracker Joke
Why does Father Christmas have three gardens?

—

So he can 'ho ho ho'!

Cracker Joke
What does Santa
suffer from if he
gets stuck in a
chimney?

—

Claustrophobia!

Across the Atlantic, in New York, a new Christmas figure was
muscling in. And to find his origins we must first return to 1624.

In 1624, the Dutch established a trading post on the southern tip
of what is now Manhattan Island and called it New Amsterdam.
They brought with them the patron saint of Old Amsterdam, St
Nicholas or, as they knew him, Sint Nikolaas or Sinter Klaas.
Almost as soon as he arrived, though, Sinter Klaas had to go
underground because the official church of New Amsterdam was
the Protestant Dutch Reform Church, and they had no truck
with Catholic saints. Accordingly, those who wished to celebrate
St Nicholas had to do so discreetly and in private.

When the British took over in 1664 and New Amsterdam
became New York, the authorities' approach to Christmas
became more relaxed. These English settlers came from the
England of Charles II, not of the Puritanical Oliver Cromwell,
and they celebrated Christmas in a suitably traditional fashion
with the jolly, non-religious English Father Christmas at the
heart of it. In fact, as they were free from the apron strings of
the Mother country, New Yorkers rather overdid it and by the
middle of the 18th century Christmas had become a time of
over-indulgence, drunkenness and licentious behaviour.

The New York gentry, in other words the Dutch, eventually
decided that something must be done to clean up Christmas and
to stop people misbehaving in the streets. They wanted to create
a Christmas where home and family were the focus. The old
pagan English Father Christmas, who had by now become quite
cosmopolitan, must be sobered up and made respectable. And so
they turned to St Nicholas.

Over time, more immigrants had been arriving from Europe, all
with their own version of St Nicholas, including a Swiss German
version called Santi-Chlaus. By the closing years of the 18th
century it appears that the jolly English Father Christmas was
becoming intermingled with the American Sinter Klaas, and it
does not take a huge stretch of the imagination to conclude that,
   in English-speaking New York, Sinter Klaas and Santi-Chlaus
      gradually became anglicised as Santa Claus.

Santa Claus first appears in print in 1773 in the *New York Gazette,* printed on Wall Street. The newspaper's owner, the English-born journalist James Rivington, writes that 'Christmas is being celebrated here with the usual Dutch festivities, including the appearance of St A. Claus.' Later that year, in the same publication, this appeared: 'Last Monday, the anniversary of St Nicholas, otherwise called Santa Claus, was celebrated at Protestant Hall, at Mr Waldron's; where a great number of sons of the ancient saint celebrated the day with great joy and festivity.' And then again, the following year, 1774: 'Monday next, being the anniversary of Saint Nicholas, will be celebrated by the descends of the ancient Dutch Families.'

John Pintard Jr

St Nicholas was ready to step back into the light, and his cause was taken up by a New York merchant from a Huguenot background called John Pintard Jr, who had a fascination with the history of New York, and in particular its Dutch origins. He was already responsible for the establishing of George Washington's birthday, the Fourth of July and Columbus Day as national holidays, and now he was determined to have St Nicholas declared patron saint of New York. In this he was unsuccessful but, not to be deterred, he made St Nicholas the patron saint of his new venture, the New-York Historical Society, which he founded in 1804. The aim of the society was to revive interest in New York's aristocratic roots, to remind callow, modern New Yorkers of a gentler time when the fast-paced, money-grubbing city was an upstanding and cultivated place called New Amsterdam, and that to be a genuine New Yorker you really had to be a New Amsterdammer. This was the toast at a New-York Historical Society dinner in 1809: 'To the memory of St Nicholas. May the virtuous habits and simple manners of our Dutch ancestors be not lost in the luxuries and refinements of the present time.'

'Without Washington Irving there would be no Santa Claus.'

Charles W. Jones

Washington Irving

At that same dinner, a young writer called Washington Irving was nominated for membership of the Society. Irving (who was born on the same day as the end of the American Revolution in 1783 and consequently named after the hero of the Revolution, George Washington) was a man with a keen sense of humour, who enjoyed gently ribbing the Society's somewhat stuffy members and their romanticised view of Dutch history in New York.

To this purpose Irving, his brother William, and brother-in-law James Kirke Paulding (nothing to do with the Captain of the Star Ship *Enterprise*, but reputed to be the author of the tongue-twisting rhyme 'Peter Piper picked a peck of pickled peppers'), brought out a satirical magazine called *Salmagundi*, which lampooned the culture and politics of New York. It was in Salmagundi that Irving first applied the name Gotham City to New York City, after discovering a village in England called Gotham where the villagers had feigned stupidity in order to deter bad King John from building himself a residence there – Gotham City, of course, would go on to become the home town of the fearless Caped Crusader, Batman.

On St Nicholas' Day 1809, Washington Irving, writing under the pseudonym Diedrich Knickerbocker, published a satirical history of New York called *A History of New York from the Beginning of the World to the End of the Dutch Dynasty*, in which he poked fun at some of the more pompous old New York families and their pride in their 'Dutch' heritage, including their devotion to St Nicholas.

In his History, Irving alludes to St Nicholas some 25 times, suggesting he be declared 'the tutelar saint of this ancient city' (New York) and telling of how the saint presided as the figurehead of the *Goede Vrouw*, the first immigrant ship to arrive in New Amsterdam, how his name was given to the first church to be built within the walls of the colony, and how St Nicholas' Day was traditionally observed.

'At this early period was
instituted that pious ceremony,
still religiously observed in all
our ancient families of the right
breed, of hanging up a stocking in
the chimney on St Nicholas Eve;
which stocking is always found in
the morning miraculously filled;
for the good St Nicholas has
ever been a great giver of gifts,
particularly to children.'

He also supplies St Nicholas with a number of the characteristics
we now associate with Santa Claus, including the ability to fly
over the tree tops and his tendency for dropping presents for the
children down the chimney.

'… in the sylvan days of New Amsterdam
the good St Nicholas would often make
his appearance in his beloved city of a
holiday afternoon, riding jollily among
the tree tops or over the roofs of the
houses, now and then drawing forth
magnificent presents from his breeches
pockets and dropping them down the
chimneys of his favorites.'

Irving's History and his depictions of St Nicholas were written in
jest and he even gives St Nicholas a gesture to show that the saint
is in on the joke.

'... and when St Nicholas had smoked his pipe, he twisted it in his hatband, and laying his finger beside his nose gave the astonished Van Kortlandt a very significant look ...'

In other words St Nicholas knows that both he and the story are a work of fiction but goes along with the pretence so as not to spoil the fun. This is a significant characteristic that will remain central to the legend of Father Christmas for ever – as grown-ups we think we know that Father Christmas does not exist, but for the sake of the children we pretend that he does.

Extraordinarily enough, the grandees of New York took Irving's History of New York extremely seriously. Irving's pseudonym, Knickerbocker, became synonymous with the New York Dutch American aristocracy and the short knee-length pantaloons they wore, while New York's baseball team, founded in the 1840s, took the name the New York Knickerbockers, or 'Knicks' for short. Solemn histories of New York were written that quoted parts of Irving's *History* as fact, even though a little research would have shown that St Nicholas didn't come to New Amsterdam on the first immigrant ship and the first church in New Amsterdam was not dedicated to St Nicholas. It just shows how we all believe what we want to believe.

Well, John Pintard Jr very much wanted to believe in St Nicholas and would not allow the saint and his importance to New York to be laughed off. For the inaugural New-York Historical Society St Nicholas anniversary dinner held on 6 December 1810, John Pintard had an artist friend, Dr Alexander Anderson, known as the Father of American Wood-engravers, design a woodcut for the occasion. This was to be the very first illustration of St Nicholas ever seen in America. The saint is shown in his role as the bringer of presents, standing next to a fireplace with stockings full of presents hanging either side, fruits and toys for the good little girl standing on the mantlepiece above it, a bunch of birch twigs for the tearful little bad boy. The woodcut is inscribed with a poem in both Dutch and English, which Pintard claims he learnt from a Dutch lady of 87 years old. The Dutch poem beings with the words 'Sancte Claus, goed, heylig man', while the English starts as follows:

Saint Nicholas, good holy man!
Put on the Tabard, best you can,
Go, clad therewith, to Amsterdam,
From Amsterdam to Hispanje,
Where apples bright of Oranje ...

So is that why we always find an orange or tangerine in our stocking? As a tribute to the Dutch royal House of Orange?

And another thing. St Nicholas is dressed in his bishop's robes and although the woodcut is uncoloured, St Nicholas' bishop's robes were known to be red. This is why Santa's coat is red. Very little to do with Coca Cola, as I will explain later.

Santa Claus is finally coming together. The next stage in his development occurred in 1821, with the publication by New York publisher William B. Gilley of the first lithographed book in America, *The Children's Friend Number III*. Although it is subtitled 'A New Year's Present for the Little Ones from Five to Twelve, Part III', the text for the first time refers to Santa Claus coming on Christmas Eve rather than New Year's Eve, which in some countries he originally did. And it shows Santa, in both the text and illustrations, riding a sleigh drawn by reindeer.

Old Santeclaus with much delight
His reindeer drives this frosty night,
O'er chimney tops, and tracks of snow,
To bring his yearly gifts to you.
The steady friend of virtuous youth,
The friend of duty, and of truth,
Each Christmas eve he joys to come
Where love and peace have made their home.
Through many houses he has been,
And various beds and stockings seen …

The author of the text and the illustrator are both unknown, and so we have no knowledge of where the idea for a sleigh drawn by reindeer came from, but there they are.

We have already heard how the Norse god Odin influenced the character of Father Christmas. Could it be that the Norse god Thor, who rode through the sky in a chariot pulled by two horned goats called Gnasher and Snarler, was the inspiration behind the idea of a sleigh drawn by reindeer? With their antlers, reindeer are not dissimilar to horned goats.

Perhaps we will never know. But whoever this anonymous author and his illustrator were we owe them a lot. Their legacy is timeless.

Cracker Joke
What do you call
a blind reindeer?
—
No idea!

'Twas the Night Before Christmas'

We now come to one of the best-known poems in the English language, a poem that, perhaps more than any other work, has been credited with creating the Santa Claus we know today.

The poem's proper title is 'A Visit from St Nicholas' but it is usually known by its first line 'Twas the night before Christmas'. First published anonymously in 1823 in the Tory Sentinel in upstate New York, it was later attributed to Clement Clarke Moore, a member of the New-York Historical Society and owner of a large country estate on Manhattan Island called Chelsea, after the Royal Chelsea Hospital for retired army personnel in London. Moore's maternal grandfather, who purchased the estate in 1750, had been a British army officer, while Moore's father was the Episcopal Bishop of New York who gave communion to Founding Father and star of his own musical Alexander Hamilton as Hamilton lay on his deathbed after his fateful duel with future Vice President Aaron Burr.

In 1821, our hero Clement Clarke Moore donated some of his land in Chelsea for an Episcopal school called the General Theological Seminary, which he set up with his friend, the New-York Historical Society founder John Pintard Jr. Moore then appointed himself Professor of Oriental and Greek Literature, Divinity and Biblical Learning. And as well as being a violinist, organist, architect and poet, Moore also compiled America's first Greek and Hebrew Lexicon.

I am telling you all this to show that Clement Clarke Moore was not only a member of New York's elite but a man of serious academic and intellectual substance. And yet what is he most remembered for? Santa Claus.

He might not even have been remembered for that had not fate taken a hand. He allegedly wrote 'Twas the Night Before Christmas' solely for his children and never intended for it to be published, but it seems that a family friend, who had asked for a copy of the poem to read to his own children, sent it anonymously to the *Troy Sentinel* and it instantly became a huge favourite with children all over America. Moore, who wanted to be known for his scholarly work, refused to acknowledge authorship of the poem until more than twenty years later in 1844 when, at the request of his children, he included it in a collection of his poems.

Clement Clarke Moore claimed to have got much of the inspiration for his St Nicholas from talking to his Dutch gardener and then taking a sleigh ride into town to do his Christmas shopping on a snowy day. And as a member of the New-York Historical Society he had attended the St Nicholas anniversary dinner in 1810, where he had no doubt picked up some ideas from both John Pintard Jr and Washington Irving. He would probably have read *The Children's Friend*, too.

Let's analyse the poem briefly to see where Clement Clarke Moore might have got his concept of St Nicholas from.

Twas the night before Christmas, when all through the house

Not a creature was stirring, not even a mouse;

The stockings were hung by the chimney with care,

In hopes that St Nicholas soon would be there …

The action takes place on Christmas Eve, rather than St Nicholas Eve or New Year's Eve. This idea was first mooted in *The Children's Friend*, published in 1821. The stockings were hung by the chimney, as mentioned in Washington Irving's History of New York, and as illustrated in Dr Alexander Anderson's woodcut of St Nicholas commissioned for the New-York Historical Society's dinner in 1810.

When what to my wondering eyes should appear, But a miniature sleigh, and eight tiny reindeer …

If Moore wrote the poem while on a sleigh ride into New York as he claimed, then this would explain the sleigh. And a sleigh drawn by reindeer also appeared in *The Children's Friend*. Was the idea for having eight reindeer derived from the Viking god Odin's eight-legged horse Sleipnir?

And he whistled, and shouted, and called them by name;

'Now, Dasher! Now, Dancer! Now, Prancer and Vixen!

On, Comet! On Cupid! On, Donder and Blitzen!

Where do the names come from? Well, the names Donder and Blitzen appear in the original Dutch in Irving's *History of New York* as Dunder and Blixum, meaning thunder and lightning, a common oath in the Dutch language. The other names were most probably chosen by the author to fit the metre of the poem – and no doubt for their alliterative effect, as in Vixen, which neatly rhymes with Blitzen.

Cracker Joke
Why did no one buy Donder and Blitzen at the Christmas Market?

—

They were two deer.

Rudolph, he of the red nose and the most famous reindeer of
them all, came along much later, in 1939, the creation of a young
advertising copywriter called Robert Lewis May as we have
already learned.

Now let's examine Clement Clarke Moore's description of
St Nicholas.

Down the chimney St Nicholas came with a bound …

… He was dressed all in fur, from his head to his foot,

And his clothes were all tarnished with ashes and soot;

A bundle of toys he had flung on his back,

And he looked like a peddler just opening his pack.

His eyes – how they twinkled! his dimples how merry!

His cheeks were like roses, his nose like a cherry!

His droll little mouth was drawn up like a bow,

And the beard of his chin was as white as the snow …

He had a broad face and a little round belly,

That shook, when he laughed like a bowlful of jelly …

St Nicholas is no longer a stern bishop but a jolly figure much more akin to the English Father Christmas, with a white beard, a cheery red face and a belly, so perhaps Moore was combining New York's two Christmas figures to create a more jovial fellow for his children. One difference, though, which is not often commented on, is that he is a tiny figure in a miniature sleigh – which maybe explains how he could fit down the chimney. And the next line reads:

He was chubby and plump,
a right jolly old elf …

So Moore's St Nicholas was an elf – could this be where the idea for Santa's little elves came from? We will look into that in a moment.

Towards the end of the poem St Nicholas makes the same gesture that Washington Irving has him make in *The History of New York*, touching his nose to indicate that he is in on the secret – this is all imaginary, but don't tell the little ones.

He spoke not a word, but went straight
to his work,

And filled all the stockings; then turned
with a jerk,

And laying his finger aside of his nose,

And giving a nod, up the chimney he rose …

'Twas the Night Before Christmas' defines our vision of Father Christmas and his role in almost every way, and the poem proved so hugely popular, not just in America but in England and beyond, that the character described in it became the accepted idea of Santa Claus across much of the world.

Thomas Nast

In 1863, cartoonist Thomas Nast, sometimes called the 'Father of the American Cartoon', created the first of what have come to be recognised as the defining images of Santa Claus in an illustration for the cover of the 3 January 1863 edition of *Harper's Weekly*. Called Santa Claus in Camp, the picture show Santa Claus visiting a Unionist military camp during the Civil War, and in the background there is a sign saying 'Welcome Santa Claus'. Most of the elements from Clement Clarke Moore's poem are there: the sleigh, the reindeer, the furry hat and tunic, the long white beard. The only difference is that Moore's little elf has become a full-grown man.

In the 1863 Christmas issue of *Harper's Weekly* Nast shows Santa Claus with a sack of presents on his back, tiptoeing past two sleeping children in bed – the first time he has been seen with his sack, as foretold in 'Twas the Night Before Christmas'.

A bundle of toys he had flung on his back, and he looked like a peddler just opening his pack.

Nast went on to develop his vision of Santa Claus in *Harper's Weekly* over the next twenty years. And not only did he show us what Santa looked like, he told us where he lived and had his workshop. With the development of the postal system, children were being encouraged to write letters to Santa Claus and they needed to know where to send them. Nast worked out that if Santa was using reindeer, which are found in far northern lands near to the Arctic, then he must come from there. Expeditions to the Arctic were big news at the time, with the adventures of people like John Franklin and James Clark Ross gripping the readers of *Harper's Weekly*, but no one had yet reached the North Pole, so it remained a place of magic and mystery, somewhere that Santa Claus might well live undiscovered. And the Norse gods, who as we know were part of Santa's ancestry, were also thought to live in the Arctic north. To Thomas Nast, it all pointed to the fact that Santa Claus lived at the North Pole.

For the 4 January 1879 issue of *Harper's Weekly* Nast drew a picture of a young girl posting a letter addressed to 'St Claus, North Pole'.

Santa Claus now had an address. In 1866, Nast produced a double-page woodcut called Santa Claus and His Works that was printed in the 29 December issue and showed Santa (and, for the first time, Mrs Claus) at home, performing all his tasks, reading the list of good and bad children, making toys, decorating the Christmas tree and delivering presents.

In 1869, a chap called George P. Webster published a poem called 'Santa Claus and his Works', complete with seven of Thomas Nast's illustrations from Harper's Weekly, this time in colour, and each of them showing Santa Claus in a red coat with white trimmings. And Webster confirms Santa's address for us.

In a nice little city called Santa Claus-ville,

With its houses and church at the foot of the hill

Lives jolly old Santa Claus; day after day

He works and he whistles the moments away.

His home through the long summer months, you must know,

Is near the North Pole, in the ice and the snow.

In 1916 the American author and illustrator Norman Rockwell began a series of paintings of Santa Claus for the cover of the *Saturday Evening Post* which showed Santa almost exactly as we now picture him, the jolly, chubby old man with a bushy white beard and big red gown described by the *Oxford English Dictionary* at the beginning of this chapter.

Norman Rockwell's paintings, Clement Clarke Moore's poem and Thomas Nast's illustrations all made it across the Atlantic to Britain, where they became as popular as they were in America. And they changed the British Christmas, just as they had changed the American Christmas. People started giving presents on Christmas Eve rather than on New Year's Eve as they had done previously. And they put up stockings. The Father Christmas of Charles Dickens' *A Christmas Carol* and the Santa Claus of Clement Clarke Moore, Thomas Nast and Norman Rockwell merged into the jolly Christmas figure in the red suit with the white beard and the big belly who delivers presents down the chimney and rides on a sleigh pulled by reindeer that we know and love today. The only difference is that in Britain people tend to call him Father Christmas while in America they prefer Santa Claus.

Santa's Pipe

One prop that Washington Irving, Clement Clarke Moore and Thomas Nast all gave Santa which has not survived the test of time is his pipe.

The stump of a pipe he held tight in his teeth,

And the smoke, it encircled his head like a wreath …

Santa gradually lost his pipe as the 19th century progressed and by the 20th century it had pretty much disappeared. Thomas Nast drew a number of images of Santa with a pipe but also drew many images of him without one. There are almost no images of 20th-century Santa with the pipe. He seems to have given up smoking naturally, with neither the health lobby nor Political Correctness being to blame but rather the fact that illustrators simply didn't feel the need to put the pipe in – its absence certainly doesn't detract from the powerful imagery.

A gentle controversy blew up, though, in 2012 when a Canadian author, Pamela McColl, published a version of 'Twas the Night Before Christmas' without the lines that refer to Santa's pipe (quoted above). To add possible insult to injury she put on the cover 'Edited by Santa Claus for the benefit of children of the 21st century'.

What some saw as just a common-sense updating of Santa for an age where smoking is seen as a bad thing that should not be associated with a beloved children's character, others saw as censorship and an intolerable interference with a much-loved classic work of literature. You decide.

Cracker Joke
Why did Santa give up his pipe?

—

It was bad for his elf!

Milk or Sherry?

And if you are going to criticise Santa's life-style then there might well be a case for getting Santa to moderate his diet a little in order to get rid of that tummy. Less of the mince pies and sherry, more of the reindeer's carrots, perhaps.

The tradition for leaving out little snacks for Father Christmas on Christmas Eve most probably comes from the Germanic custom of providing food for Father Winter, and the Norse practice of leaving out something for Odin's eight-legged horse Sleipnir in the hope of being spared a harsh winter. In North America, there is a school of thought that the custom may have been reinforced during the era of the Great Depression when children were encouraged by their parents to share with others.

Santa's Treats

The treats on offer to Santa Claus vary around the world.

In Britain, it is traditional to leave out a mince pie and a glass of sherry or ginger wine to warm Father Christmas against the chill weather.

In North America, they are a little more health conscious and leave Santa a fortifying glass of milk with a plate of chocolate chip or gingerbread cookies.

In Ireland, what else could it be but a mince pie and a pint of Guinness?

In the Scandinavian countries, Santa gets a bowl of hearty rice porridge, possibly with a cup of coffee in Sweden or maybe a jug of beer in Norway.

In Latvia, the treat on offer is a *piparkukas*, which is a type of spicy or peppered gingerbread biscuit that is often hung on the Christmas tree.

The Dutch are much more concerned with the poor reindeer and tend to leave carrots (good for seeing at night) along with some hay and a bowl of water.

The French are the same and leave carrots for the reindeer, although they do put out biscuits for Santa too.

In Italy, Santa gets a clementine while the reindeer get some hay.

In Germany and Switzerland, poor Santa gets nothing at all. Instead children are encouraged to write him a letter outlining their hopes and fears, and in return the Christkind will leave a small gift.

In the southern hemisphere it's summer-time, of course, so Santa prefers something cool, especially as he has to race around in that heavy red coat. In Australia, for instance, which is one of his first stops, they speed him on his way with a glass of the amber nectar (beer) and a plate of biscuits, plus some carrots for the reindeer.

In Chile, Santa can stock up on some delicious *pan de pascua* (Christmas bread), which is a type of sponge cake made with candied fruit, ginger and honey.

Santa's Elves

Everyone knows that Santa Claus is helped in his work by elves.

Cracker Joke
What do you call Santa's little helpers?
—
Subordinate clauses!

They design and make toys for children, look after the reindeer and guard the secret location of Santa's home at the North Pole. Most important, they draw up the list of good and bad children so that Santa knows who to give presents to.

It is this last responsibility that gives us a clue as to where elves might come from. Elves in fact are related to a whole body of mythical creatures from folklore like pixies, fairies and goblins, the Irish leprechaun, the Swedish tomte and the Danish nisse. In Norse mythology elves were diminutive, gnome-like creatures with magical powers who were believed to guard the home from evil.

In pagan communities good or bad harvests were thought to be in the gift of capricious spirits, and during winter solstice ceremonies presents of food and drink were offered to these spirits in the hope of ensuring a fruitful growing season. In the same way, Norse elf figures would decide one's fate according to whether they thought you had been good or bad. If you were bad then the elves would play tricks on you such as turning your milk sour, stealing things like your breakfast sausage or your hat, tangling up your hair, putting a spell on you or sitting on your head and giving you nightmares – indeed, the word elf comes from the Old English *oelf* which in turn is derived from the Old Germanic *alb*, meaning nightmare. In fact mischievous elves were blamed for any kind of bad luck or unexplained misfortune, and in order to placate them and keep them from their mischief it was customary to leave a bowl of porridge out for them overnight, a practice we still observe when leaving out a treat for Santa Claus on Christmas Eve.

So how did Santa Claus get muddled up with these mercurial creatures? Well, elves were no doubt brought to America by immigrants from Northern Europe in the 18th and 19th centuries, along with fabled Scandinavian characters such as the Swedish *tomte* and Danish *nisse*, and so would have been familiar to 19th-century Americans who were interested in such things. Perhaps the most famous 'elf' of all, at least for immigrants from England, would have been William Shakespeare's Puck from *A Midsummer Night's Dream*. And in 1819 Washington Irving wrote a widely proclaimed short story about Rip van Winkle, a farmer who has a sleeping spell cast over him by mysterious gnome-like figures from the Dead while wandering in the Catskill Mountains.

Equally, Santa's ancestor St Nicholas was known to have helpers in his task of bringing gifts to children, companions whose job it was to be the bad guy and punish the naughty children. They were rather alarming figures such as Knecht Ruprecht (Servant Rupert) in Germany or the half-goat, half-demon Krampus in Austria or the Dutch Zwarte Piet, Black Peter.

It is more than likely that the author of the influential Christmas poem 'Twas the Night Before Christmas', Clement Clarke Moore, would have heard of St Nicholas' Zwarte Piet in particular, since St Nicholas was the patron saint of the New-York Historical Society of which Moore was a member. So, in the same way that elves were known about, so the idea of Santa's helpers was not entirely new. It just needed someone to bring the two together.

In 'Twas the Night Before Christmas', Moore does just that, describing Santa Claus as 'a right jolly old elf'. Although elf was probably used here just as a general term for any one of the tiny mythical creatures that were out there, it is the first mention anywhere of elves in a Christmas context, and may well have been what first led people to associate Santa Claus with elves, and set writers and artists off in search of these elusive little beings.

In 1855, for instance, Louisa May Alcott, the author of *Little Women*, wrote in her journal that she had finished a book of tales called 'Christmas Elves'. Unfortunately the book was never published and the manuscript was lost, so we have to wait for a couple more years to find out what role the elves actually might play in the Christmas story.

In 1857 an anonymous poem called 'The Wonders of Santa Claus' appeared in *Harper's Weekly*. Included was a verse in which we learn this about Santa Claus and his elves.

In his house upon the top of a hill,
  And almost out of sight,
He keeps a great many elves at work,
  All working with all their might,
To make a million of pretty things,
  Cakes, sugar-plums, and toys,
To fill the stockings, hung up you know
  By the little girls and boys.

Ah ha! So here, for the first time, we see that Santa's elves worked at making toys. And later in the poem we are told that when a stranger appears, Santa Claus 'orders every elf to stop' and the house and workshop and all the elves disappear into a frosty mist. Clearly, Santa Claus doesn't want the location of his workshop to be discovered. Another task for his elves.

For the first pictorial glimpse of Santa's elves at work we must turn again to Godey's *Lady Book*, the magazine, if you remember, that helped to make the Christmas tree popular in America. In 1873 their front cover showed a picture of Santa Claus issuing instructions to an army of elves who are beavering away at making toys. The heading was 'The Workshop of Santa Claus', while the caption inside stated, 'Here we have an idea of the preparations that are made to supply the young folks with toys at Christmas time'.

Although, as far as we know, no one has ever actually seen an elf, Santa's elves are commonly depicted as being small, mischievous creatures with pointy ears and pointy bobble hats, dressed up in the Christmas colours of red and green This is pretty much as they appear in Norman Rockwell's 'Santa with Elves' painting for the cover of the Saturday *Evening Post*'s 2 December 1922 edition.

And so, helped along by illustrations such as this, and by numerous children's books and Disney films, Santa's helpers have become a well-established part of Christmas.

Mrs Claus

Mrs Claus provides a good example of how Christmas has evolved along with the changes in society. In the 19th century, she was barely seen, perhaps mentioned in passing in one or two literary pieces, and her role was restricted to tending the home and overseeing the elves while Santa was away on his travels. It wasn't until 1889 that she really got into the action in any meaningful way. In a charming book called *Goody Santa Claus on a Sleigh Ride* by Katharine Lee Bates, Mrs Claus (the 'Goody' Santa Claus of the title) persuades her husband to take her with him on his rounds, in return for all her hard work, and together they enjoy many adventures in which Mrs Claus proves herself every inch his equal.

Since the 1960s Mrs Claus has begun to appear more regularly, in storybooks, on Christmas cards, in pageants and parades and school plays, at Christmas grottoes and, particularly, in films. While her appearance, rather like her husband's, has remained fairly consistent as elderly, white-haired and plumpish, her personality as a calm and kindly foil to Santa's exuberance has matured into a hands-on partner in Santa's enterprises. Her contemporary image is deftly captured in a 2016 Marks & Spencer TV advertisement in which Mrs Claus saves the day by helicoptering in from the North Pole to deliver a pair of red trainers to a young boy's exasperated big sister.

Coca-Cola's Santa

In 1931, Swedish artist Haddon Sundblom painted an image of Santa Claus for a Coca-Cola advert for the *Saturday Evening Post*. Sundblom's vision of Santa as a plump and friendly bearded fellow in a red coat was based on Clement Clarke Moore's description of Santa in his poem 'Twas the Night Before Christmas'. Fortuitously red was also the corporate colour of Coca-Cola and so the two were a perfect match. Sundblom went on to paint Santa for Coca-Cola for the next 30 years and the advertisements were seen in magazines, billboards, posters, calendars and toys all over the world, leading many people to believe that Coca-Cola had in fact invented Santa's famous red coat. As we have seen, however, the red coat was based on St Nicholas's red bishop's robes. Nonetheless, thanks to the world-wide reach of Coca-Cola, Haddon Sundblom's Santa is probably the most recognised Santa Claus of them all.

Santa's Christmas Grotto

Although both Washington Irving and Clement Clarke Moore seemed to indicate that Santa Claus was imaginary, since 1879 the children of Liverpool have known better. In 1879 the world's first ever Santa's Christmas Grotto opened in Liverpool, in Lewis's department store, and there children were able to meet Father Christmas in person and tell him what they wanted for Christmas. The idea for the grotto, which was called Christmas Fairyland, was that of entrepreneur David Lewis, who wanted a Christmas themed display to fill the exhibition hall of his store. The grotto was a cavern filled with Christmas lights and decorations, Christmas trees, lots of snow, a couple of polar bears, models of some Liverpool landmarks and, of course, the real-life Father Christmas. The idea proved a smash success and other stores soon decided to set up their own Christmas grottoes where children could meet Father Christmas and receive a toy from him.

Lewis's Christmas Fairyland grotto is still going strong in Liverpool. When Lewis's department store closed in 2010, the grotto moved across the road to the fourth floor of the Rapid Hardware store. It now takes place in the city's St John's indoor market.

Although generally accepted as the first Santa's Christmas Grotto, Lewis's Christmas Fairyland may have been pipped by Houlden Brothers of Nicolson Street in Edinburgh, who decorated their emporium with a Fairy Christmas Tree and Magic Grotto in 1870 – although there is no record of Father Christmas himself putting in an appearance.

In 1882, Thomas Nast created a picture for *Harper's Weekly* captioned 'The Shrine of St Nicholas – We are all good children'. It showed a group of children gazing ardently at Santa Claus, who is sitting on a box inscribed with the words 'Christmas Box 1882 St Nicholas North Pole'. And they are all gathered in what looks like a cave – which could be mistaken for a grotto – bedecked with stalactites or icicles, some of them in the shape of slightly sinister faces.

By the end of the 19th century, Christmas grottoes had become popular in America, Australia and New Zealand as well as Britain.

USA

The best-known Christmas grotto in America is Santaland at Macy's in New York. In the 1860s Macy's became the first department store in the US to put up special window displays for Christmas, and it was at Macy's that Santa Claus first put in a personal appearance in 1870, although he had no grotto at that time. Since 1924, Santa has led the annual Thanksgiving Day Parade to Macy's flagship store in Herald Square before taking up residence in Santaland until Christmas Eve.

Australia and New Zealand

Father Christmas made his first personal appearance south of the Equator at the Magic Cave in John Martin's Department Store in Adelaide, South Australia, in 1896. John Martin's closed in 1996 but the Magic Cave was inherited by the David Jones store that replaced John Martin's, and Father Christmas still appears there after the Adelaide Christmas Pageant. This is the biggest pageant in the southern hemisphere, and first took place in 1933. It usually happens on the second or third Saturday in November.

And so we arrive at the big day ...

Christmas Day is the day on which Christians celebrate the Birth of Jesus Christ, and in Christian countries is a public holiday. Christmas Day is also the day on which most people, certainly in Britain and America, enjoy their Christmas meal and open their presents.

In some countries, people eat their main Christmas meal on New Year's Eve, but in Britain and America, Canada, Australia and New Zealand, and other countries settled by immigrants from Britain, it is customary to have it at lunch time on Christmas Day. Each country has its specialities - in Britain, for instance, the traditional ingredients are turkey and Christmas pudding.

Here are some Christmas specialities for which countries around the world are renowned

USA and Canada: Eggnog

Australia and New Zealand: Fresh fruit Pavlova

France: Caviar, oysters, pâté de foie gras, Champagne

Germany: Stollen, gingerbread, Glühwein (mulled wine)

Italy: Panettone (sweet bread)

Spain: Chicken noodle soup, *torrons* (baked sweet made with honey, nuts and egg)

Portugal: *Consoada* (baked codfish), *Bolo Rei* (fruit cake)

Poland: *Pierogi* (stuffed dumplings)

Eastern Europe: Carp (meat free meal)

Scandinavian countries: Rice pudding, *glogg* (mulled wine)

Puerto Rico: *Coquito* (eggnog with made with coconut milk and rum)

Columbia: *Natilla* (a creamy custard dessert with coconut, cheese and raisins)

Mexico: Tamales with chicken (steamed corn cakes stuffed with meat, fruits, vegetables or chillies)

Japan: Kentucky Fried Chicken, strawberry sponge cake

The Christmas Meal

'The old halls of castles and manor-houses resounded with the harp and the Christmas carol, and their ample boards groaned under the weight of hospitality.'

Washington Irving: Old Christmas

An important component of Christmas day is feasting. At least it is for me, and millions like me. We can't help it, it is in our DNA. Since the dawn of time our ancestors have feasted in midwinter.

As so often, it is all to do with the seasons. Back in time when most people were farmers and worked on the land, everything revolved around the rhythm of the seasons. Come the winter months, it gets cold and the grass stops growing. Livestock must be brought in from the fields, housed in barns and fed on hay. Hay was expensive and in limited supply, which meant that many animals were slaughtered so they wouldn't have to be fed and sheltered. Hence there was a sudden glut of fresh meat which needed to be eaten. Likewise wines and beer that had been fermenting over the summer would be ready for drinking.

In days of yore, the feasting was a village affair. The whole community would come together and contribute to the spoils. In medieval times, the squire or lord of the manor would fling open his doors and invite the villagers to feast at his table on meats and game of every kind – beef, lamb, venison, ham, partridge, pheasant, goose, all washed down with plenty of ale.

For a while in the 17th century, Christmas, and the feasting associated with Christmas, were banned by the Puritans, and by the time Christmas returned with the Restoration of Charles II to the throne it had become rather more low key. In the 18th century, farming communities began to dissolve as industrialisation moved people off the land and into the towns, and the Christmas meal became more of a family affair, rather than a gargantuan communal feast such as was enjoyed in the Tudor years. The Victorians sought to restore many of the old Christmas traditions, and while they baulked at some of the more vulgar elements associated with Merrie England, they eagerly embraced the family feast. And in this way the Christmas meal evolved into the family occasion it is today.

The Christmas Meal in Britain

'It was a regular Christmas dinner, with turkeys,
Baron of Beef, Plum Pudding & Mince Pies.''
Queen Victoria's journal, 25 December 1843

In Britain, the traditional Christmas meal consists of something along these lines. Turkey, sausages wrapped in bacon, roast potatoes and Brussels sprouts, followed by Christmas pudding and mince pies. How did that all come about?

Turkey

Today nine out of ten Britons have a turkey for their Christmas meal. But it was not always thus. Until about the middle of the 20th century it was more common to have a native bird such as a goose at Christmas, or possibly a pheasant or a pigeon. Birds were plentiful and could be hunted, unlike many animals such as deer or boar which, in medieval England, were the preserve of the king or local landowners. Even a goose could be expensive and poorer families in Georgian and Victorian times would often join a 'goose club' at the beginning of the year and put a few pennies aside every week towards saving for their Christmas bird. If they didn't have their own oven, which many people didn't, they would take it to the local baker to be cooked.

Or you might be lucky and get invited up to the Big House to share in a roast boar's head decorated with a sprig of holly.

Turkeys were introduced into Britain in the 1520s by a Yorkshireman called William Strickland, who brought back six live turkeys that he had purchased from some native Americans while on a voyage to the New World with Sebastian Cabot. Henry VIII subsequently became the first English king to enjoy turkey and it was soon fashionable among the nobility to have turkey at the dinner table instead of peacocks, which were not only smaller and tougher to eat, but could now be preserved decorative purposes.

Cracker Joke
Why did they
need the turkey
in the band?
—
It had the
drumsticks!

In 1843, Charles Dickens popularised the idea of a turkey for Christmas in his novella *A Christmas Carol*, in which he has the guilt-ridden humbug Ebenezer Scrooge give a huge turkey to his ill-used clerk Bob Cratchit and his family in place of their usual goose.

Edward VII apparently enjoyed his Christmas turkey, and what the royal family enjoyed soon everyone enjoyed. Turkey was still expensive, however, and remained a luxury for most people right up until the 1950s, when the use of refrigerators became widespread and turkeys could be stored safely and didn't have to be eaten all in one sitting. Once it was affordable, turkey became a favourite, not least because being such a big bird it could feed plenty of hungry mouths.

Today some 10 million turkeys are eaten at Christmas-time in Britain every year.

Sausages wrapped in bacon ('pigs in blankets')

Like the turkey, these little bacon-wrapped sausages came from
America but much more recently. They were invented – or at least
made popular – by an American cook called Betty Crocker who
included them in her 1957 cookbook *Betty Crocker's Cooking for Kids*.

Roast potatoes

Potatoes came from South America originally and were
introduced into Ireland and then Britain by Sir Walter Raleigh
in the 16th century. They proved cheap and easy to grow and
soon became a staple diet. They were first roasted in the early
19th century when enclosed ovens became more widespread –
previously meats had been cooked on a spit above an open fire
while potatoes were boiled separately.

Brussels sprouts

Brussels sprouts cause more arguments at the British Christmas
table than almost anything else. Loved by some and hated
by others, especially children, these little mini cabbages were
introduced to Britain from Germany by the Hanoverian court.
First cultivated by the Romans, they were widely grown in
northern European countries such as Holland and what became
Belgium – hence the name. Prince Albert loved his sprouts and
is largely responsible for their popularity, as with so many other
aspects of the British Christmas. Add to that the fact that they are
a winter vegetable and ready to eat at Christmas-time and it is
clear why sprouts are the obvious choice. They are also incredibly
good for you – one sprout contains more vitamin C than an
orange – and they are also said to aid fertility.

Cracker Joke
What's the
most popular
Christmas wine?

—

'I don't like
Brussels sprouts!'

Christmas Pudding

Like the turkey, the traditional British Christmas pudding was championed by Queen Victoria and Prince Albert. This is one Christmas tradition that was home grown, however, and did not come from Germany. There is a tale, probably concocted by the Victorians in their effort to promote plum pudding for Christmas, about how the German-born George I got the name the 'pudding king' after he demanded traditional English plum pudding for his first English Christmas feast, probably as a way of bonding with his new subjects.

Among ordinary folk the idea of having a plum pudding for Christmas was again made popular by Charles Dickens in *A Christmas Carol*.

'In half a minute Mrs Cratchit entered – flushed, but smiling proudly – with the pudding, like a speckled cannon ball, so hard and firm, blazing in half a quartern of ignited brandy, and bedight with Christmas Holly stuck into the top. Oh, what a wonderful pudding!'

Charles Dicken, *A Christmas Carol*, 19th December 1843

The Christmas pudding comes down to us from medieval England and began life as a pottage, which was a kind of thick soup or stew produced by slowly boiling vegetables and grains, and sometimes meat or fish, in a large cauldron over a wood fire. Pottage was a popular dish because you could throw anything into it that was available, and since there was plenty of wood in medieval England the fire could be kept burning to keep the pottage simmering all day long, so that there was always hot food available. Sometimes, in wealthier households, the pottage was livened up with spices, and sweetened with dried fruits and wine, and on festive occasions it might be doused in brandy and served flambéed.

Another way of serving the pottage was to make it into a pudding by thickening it with breadcrumbs, ground almonds and egg yolk, adding dried fruit, packing it into an animal stomach, rather like you do a sausage, and leaving it to stand. In this way it would keep for longer.

The most common type of dried fruit used as a sweetener in puddings was the prune, or dried plum, which was grown in England and was thus cheaper and more readily available than currants, sultanas and raisins, which had to be imported. Eventually a pottage with any kind of dried fruit in it became known as a plum pottage or a plum pudding.

In the 17th century, the pudding cloth came along to replace animal intestines, and puddings became the food of choice since they could conveniently be left to cook on their own all day and they could be made from almost any ingredients. As new spices for meat became available, cooks began to divide their puddings into savoury and sweet – steak pudding or plum pudding.

Plum pudding was regarded as something of a treat and was served at Harvest Festival or in the run-up to Christmas, or maybe at the start of the Christmas meal to line the stomach before the main course. As it developed into more of a sweet dish so it began to be eaten after the main course – as what we now call a 'sweet', 'dessert' or 'pudding'.

There are many myths and tales surrounding how the plum pudding came to be associated with Christmas. One such tale involves a decree put out by the Roman Catholic Church in the mid-16th century that 'pudding should be made on the 25th Sunday after Trinity, that it be prepared with 13 ingredients to represent Christ and the 12 apostles, and that every family member stir it in turn from east to west to honour the Magi and their supposed journey in that direction'.

Indeed, the Collect for the 25th Sunday after Trinity in the 16th century *Book of Common Prayer* reads: 'Stir up, we beseech thee, oh Lord, the wills of thy faithful people, that they plenteously bringing forth the fruit of good works, may of thee be plenteously rewarded, through Jesus Christ our Lord, Amen.' The 25th Sunday after Trinity, which occurs roughly one month before Christmas at the beginning of Advent, became known as 'Stir Up Sunday' and it was popular with the Victorians.

It was a Victorian cook, Eliza Acton from Tonbridge in Kent, who first specifically called her festive plum pudding a Christmas pudding, in her *Modern Cookery for Private Families*, which came out in 1845. In this, one of the first cookbooks ever published, Acton, described by Delia Smith as 'the best writer of recipes in the English language', lays out a recipe for 'The Author's Christmas Pudding'. This recipe is now regarded as the standard for Christmas pudding, and includes all the traditional ingredients: raisins and sultanas, spices, suet, flour, eggs, brown sugar and brandy.

Because plum pudding is steeped in alcohol, it can be preserved for months. When it comes to be served up, it is traditional to pour some more alcohol, usually brandy, over the pudding and set it alight. Depending on your point of view this either harks back to pagan fire rituals, which is why it was banned by the Puritans, or symbolises the burning passion of Christ. If you put a sprig of holly on top, again according to your preferences, this can be viewed as replicating a pagan gesture to ward off evil spirits, or as Christ's crown of thorns.

It was also common practice, until quite recently, to place small trinkets into the pudding mix. Whoever found a silver coin in their serving would enjoy wealth in the coming year, a ring signified marriage and a thimble spinsterhood. What it signified if you swallowed the trinket isn't made clear; probably a bad bout of indigestion.

Christmas Cake

Christmas cake is another form of Christmas pudding and is made from the same ingredients. Wealthier households would cut a chunk off the plum pudding and spread a layer of almond marzipan on it as a special delicacy.

Mince Pies

The traditional British mince pie also shares its ancestry with the Christmas pudding. Meat, poultry and fish that were slaughtered in the autumn were minced (from the Latin *minuo*, meaning to make small) and then sweetened and preserved by being wrapped in a flour 'pastry' along with dried fruit, spices, butter and wine or brandy. These 'minced meat pyes' were a useful way of pre-preparing food for the long Christmas festival to come, but the ingredients were quite expensive and they were originally a treat for the rich. They were made in all different shapes and rectangular pies were sometimes capped with a figure of the baby Jesus made out of dough to represent Jesus lying in his manger.

Over time new farming methods enabled farmers to feed their livestock more cheaply over the winter and this, along with improved preserving techniques, meant that meat didn't need to be preserved in the same way and the 'minced meat pies' were filled with just the dried fruit and no meat, becoming a purely sweet dish while retaining the name 'mince' pie. Meat finally disappeared from mince pies altogether in the Victorian era, although Eliza Acton's 1845 recipe for mincemeat did include ox tongue. Mrs Beeton was perhaps the first to concoct a mincemeat recipe without meat, in her book *Mrs Beeton's Household Management*, published in 1861.

It is said that if you eat a mince pie on every one of the twelve days of Christmas you will have good health for the next year.

Cracker Joke
Who hides in the larder at Christmas?

—

A mince spy!

Drink

Drink, specifically beer and wine, has always been an integral part of midwinter and Christmas celebrations.

Many people nowadays like to start the festivities with Champagne, which certainly gives a fizz to the proceedings. Then there is wine, of course, especially mulled wine, and fortified wines like sherry or port are always popular at Christmas. And, of course, one mustn't forget to leave a warming tot of sherry or ginger wine out for Father Christmas on Christmas Eve to wash down his mince pies.

And although beer is not so much associated with Christmas these days, it was actually drunk much more widely at midwinter festivals than wine since it was cheaper and easier to make. Those who still prefer beer at Christmas need not despair, for there is always a wide selection of limited edition English ales brought out by various micro breweries just for Christmas. Here are just a few random examples from past Christmases:

Byatt's XXXmas

Hornes Brewery's A Dickens of an Ale

Backyard Brewhouse's Bad Santa

West Berkshire's Yule Fuel

Baa Brewing's Bah Humbug

Arkells' Sir Noel

Hook Norton's Twelve Days

Great Orme's Brewdolph

And from Britain's oldest brewery,

Shepherd Neame, a simple Christmas Ale.

Of course, the ingredients of the modern Christmas meal vary from country to country, and often from region to region, depending on local custom and the type of produce available. In fact, today there are almost as many different Christmas meals as there are countries and cultures. In English-speaking nations populated by immigrants from Britain, the basics of the Christmas meal are the same, although each has its own specialities as well.

USA

The Christmas meal in America is quite similar to the British Christmas meal, although there are some subtle differences. Americans eat turkey at Thanksgiving (on the fourth Thursday in November) and therefore tend to choose a different meat, usually ham or beef, for Christmas. And although some in America like Christmas pudding, others go for pie, not mince but pumpkin, pecan or apple.

A popular Christmas drink is eggnog, known to have been enjoyed by none other than George Washington, the first President of the United States. He even had his own recipe, recorded in America's oldest continuously published periodical, *The Old Farmer's Almanac* (founded 1792). It consisted of cream, milk, brown sugar, eggs separated into yolks and whites, and one pint of brandy, half a pint of rye whiskey, half a pint of Jamaica rum and a quarter pint of sherry. The recipe ends with the advice: 'Taste frequently.' Well you'd have to, wouldn't you?

Eggnog is not so well known in Britain, although it seems to have originally been taken to America by the British, as Captain John Smith reported eggnog being enjoyed in Jamestown in 1607.

On Christmas Day 1826, eggnog caused a riot at West Point Academy in New York State when whiskey was smuggled into the academy to make eggnog and some 70 cadets got drunk. It became known as the Eggnog Riot.

Canada

Canadians stick pretty closely to the British Christmas menu
of turkey and Christmas pudding, although Quebec adds a few
French-inspired delicacies to the mix, such as *tourtière*, a meat pie
made with pork and potato, and *Bûche de Noël*, a frosted sponge
cake made of chocolate and chestnuts equivalent to a Yule log.
Some residents of Vancouver on the west coast prefer wild salmon
to turkey but all Canadians enjoy Brussels sprouts, which grow
widely in Canada, and potatoes from Prince Edward Island.
Shortbread cookies are a favourite from England, while eggnog
from the US is much enjoyed, as is mulled apple cider made from
Ontario apples.

Australia and New Zealand

Since Christmas comes in summer time, few Australians or New
Zealanders will have a hot roast Christmas meal. Cold meats,
turkey or ham, or seafood and salad are favoured, as is a barbecue
on the beach – a traditional destination is Sydney's Bondi Beach
where up to 50,000 people go to celebrate Christmas Day every
year. Christmas pudding is eaten with cold custard or ice cream
or, as an alternative, some people like a fresh fruit Pavlova. A cold
beer is usually preferred to wine.

European countries all have their own favourite Christmas
dishes, too.

France

The custom in France is to have the Christmas meal on
Christmas Eve or early on Christmas morning after midnight
service. As for ingredients there are many regional variations
but popular Christmas dishes are turkey stuffed with chestnuts,
goose, duck, smoked salmon, oysters, pâté de foie gras and french
beans cooked in garlic, all accompanied by champagne and the
best French wines. Instead of Christmas pudding many French
people like to round off the meal with a tradition from Provence
in the south of France called *Les Treize Desserts de Noël*. This
consists of thirteen different desserts in honour of Christ and the
twelve disciples, and is laid out on the table overnight lit by three
candles representing the Holy Trinity. The thirteen desserts each
have a meaning and every person has to have a small portion of
each one to ensure good luck in the coming year. The following
is a list of the basic desserts, of which, again, there are many
local variations.

Les Treize Desserts de Noël

The menu begins with two nougats which mark the passage of the winter solstice.

1)   Black nougat symbolising the dark, or evil.

2)   White nougat symbolising the light, or good.

3)   Fresh seasonal fruit, such as apples, oranges, pears, mandarins and melon, to symbolise the bounty of nature.

4)   Dates to celebrate Christ's journey out of the East.

5)   *Pompe à l'huile*, a flatbread made with olive oil. This should be broken not cut, as it symbolises the bread broken by Jesus at the Last Supper.

6)   *Calissons d'Aix* (little hugs), a fruity pastry or biscuit associated with Aix en Provence, similar in texture to marzipan and topped with ground almonds. They symbolise the gift of love, and eating a *calisson* every day is said to protect you from the plague.

7)   Candied fruits symbolise the gifts given to the baby Jesus by the Three Wise Men.

8)   *Bûche de Noël*, an imitation of the Yule log.

9)   Nougat of the Capuchins, figs stuffed with walnuts, representing the Capuchin monks.

        Finally *les quatre mendiants* or four begging friars (nuts or dried fruits of a similar colour to the habits of different orders of friar):

10)   Walnuts or hazelnuts for Augustinians,

11)   Figs for Franciscans,

12)   Raisins for Dominicans,

13)   Almonds for Carmelites.

All washed down with a glass of mulled wine. Delicious.

Germany

In Germany the typical Christmas meal features something roast, wild boar or venison perhaps, or possibly duck or goose, accompanied by kale, red cabbage and sauerkraut with potato dumplings or *Kartoffelsalat* (potato salad) and an apple and sausage stuffing. For pudding there is Christmas Stollen, preferably from Dresden, and Lebkuchen, gingerbread biscuits. A particular treat is the *Pfefferkuchenhaus*, a gingerbread cake baked in the shape of a house, inspired by the story of Hansel and Gretel.

The drink of choice at Christmas, served throughout the Christmas period and at Christmas markets, is Glühwein, a hot red wine spiced with cinnamon sticks, cloves and citrus and occasionally fortified with some other liquor such as rum or vodka.

Eastern Europe

In Eastern European countries such as Lithuania, Poland, Ukraine, the Czech Republic and Slovakia, the main Christmas meal is eaten on Christmas Eve, and because Christmas Eve is the last day of the Advent fast in the East (see Advent) the main dish is fish, as no meat is allowed. If you are in Poland, Slovakia or the Czech Republic, the fish is most likely carp. It is the custom in Eastern European countries to serve twelve courses in honour of the twelve Apostles and, indeed, the twelve months of the year. Each country has its own specialities, but what they all have in common is that they do not include meat and they are accompanied by local beers and vodkas.

In Poland, for example, the twelve courses might look something like this. Having first scattered the dining table with hay to represent the stable where Jesus was born, they begin the meal with soup. First there is a traditional Christmas red bortsch, which is a beetroot soup made of raw beets fermented in garlic and then mixed with a mushroom broth and served with *uszka*, small dumplings made from cep mushrooms and fried onions. Next comes a dried forest mushroom soup with noodles. Then comes the carp, accompanied by sauerkraut, dried mushrooms and potatoes. Then herring fillets with a vegetable salad. Then a famous Polish favourite, the Christmas version of pierogi, a dumpling stuffed with cabbage or sauerkraut or cep mushrooms. In eastern Poland, they stuff their pierogi with dried plums. Sauerkraut, you may have noticed, appears with pretty much every course and can be served in different ways: braised, as a stuffing, with mushrooms, or as a side dish with white beans or raisins. A further course is cabbage roll. This is usually stuffed with meat but at Christmas the filling is vegetarian: buckwheat, pearl barley, rice and mushrooms. Now we reach the Polish version of plum pudding, an ancient delicacy called *kutia*, which is made from wheat grains, poppy seeds, honey, dried fruits, almonds and walnuts all soaked in red wine or port. To finish there are gingerbread cookies and, to aid digestion, *susz*, a smoked fruit compote of plums, cherries, apricots, apples, pears and raisins. And it is not a bad idea to sample a portion of each course, because anyone who skips a course will die in the coming year and that would be a shame!

Scandinavian Countries

In Sweden, the main Christmas meal is eaten on Christmas Eve, with leftovers served on Christmas Day. The meal consists of a *julbord*, a festive smorgasbord of four or five courses including pickled herring, salmon dishes, boiled, smoked and pâté, hot meatballs and cold meats and rice pudding. The centre piece of the meal is the *julskinka* or Christmas ham, a dish handed down from the Aesir or Norse gods who, every night, feasted on a wild boar called Särimner. After the meal the bones and scraps would be gathered up and Särimner brought back to life again, ready for the next day's feasting. To accompany the food, Swedes enjoy glogg, a Swedish mulled wine, schnaps, a strong spirit flavoured with caraway and *julol*, a sweet dark beer brewed especially for Christmas.

Norway and Finland like pork and fish with their julbord, Denmark goes with goose or duck. For their Christmas pudding all the Scandinavians like rice pudding, which is rather more interesting than it sounds, with each country mixing up the pudding in their own way. The Norwegians, for instance, flavour their rice pudding, or *risengrynsgrøt* as they call it, with cinnamon, sugar and butter. The Danes add whipped milk, almonds, vanilla and, if they are being really indulgent, cherry sauce. In both Denmark and Norway a whole almond is hidden in the pudding and whoever finds it wins a special treat.

They all enjoy their own version of glogg (*glogi* in Finland) as well, spicing the mulled wine up with ingredients such as cinnamon, vanilla, ginger, strawberry juice, blackcurrant juice, grapefruit juice, cherry or almond liqueur.

Cracker Joke
Why did the turkey cross the road?

—

Because he wasn't chicken

Japan

Christmas came to Japan from America, and so did the idea of eating turkey at Christmas. Since turkey is hard to find in Japan, people tried eating chicken instead and in 1974 Kentucky Fried Chicken saw the main chance and ran an advert called *Kurisumasu ni wa kentakkii* or 'Kentucky for Christmas', and now some 4 million families tuck into Kentucky Fried Chicken on Christmas Day. Another favourite is Japanese Christmas cake, a sponge cake with strawberries and whipped cream.

***
Odds and Ends

Why are turkeys called turkeys when they don't come from Turkey but from America? When the English first saw a turkey they thought it was a kind of guinea fowl, such as was imported into England from Africa by merchants from Constantinople, the same merchants who had originally introduced the turkey into Europe and Asia from America. In the days when much of the East was ruled by the Ottoman Empire, centred on Turkey, anything arriving in London from the East was labelled as from Turkey, and so the new bird was called a 'turkey coq'.

And what is a turkey called in Turkey? A hindi, meaning 'from India'. This comes from the French for turkey, which is *dinde*, also meaning 'from India'. For some reason, the French thought the bird came from India, possibly because Christopher Columbus, on discovering America, thought he had found India, which is how American Indians came to be called Indians and how the West Indies became the West Indies. The Russians (*indyushka*), the Poles (*indyk*) and the Arab countries (*diiq Hindi*) all seem to be labouring under the same misconception. The Portuguese get a little closer. They call the turkey a *peru*. Nobody, it seems, calls the turkey by its rightful name, the america.

***

Cracker Joke
What do you get
if you cross Santa
with a duck?
—
A Christmas
quacker

Christmas Crackers

At the end of the Christmas meal people in Britain, Ireland and Commonwealth countries such as Australia, New Zealand and South Africa will pull crackers. Simple pleasures.

The Christmas cracker was invented by a Victorian confectioner called Tom Smith, who ran a sweet shop and factory in Goswell Road in East London. Always on the lookout for new ideas, in 1840 he travelled to Paris and came across the bon bon, a sugared almond wrapped in a twist of paper. (Bonbon later became a general French word for sweet.) He brought the bon bon back to London and began to sell it, with some success, as a novelty Christmas treat – and, indeed, the twist of paper has evolved into the sweet wrapper as we know it today. Over the next few years Tom added new elements, first inserting a love motto into the wrapper and then, inspired by the crackling of logs on a fire, adding an exciting 'crack' that detonated when the wrapping was broken. This proved a great success and Tom decided to refine the product, dropping the bon bon and instead wrapping the twist of paper around a cardboard tube in which there were little trinkets, toys or pieces of jewellery, along with the ever-present love motto. Thus was born the Christmas cracker and it proved so successful that Tom had to move production to bigger premises in Finsbury Square, where the business was to remain until 1953. After Tom died in 1880 the company was taken over by his sons, Tom, Henry and Walter, who took their father's idea and developed it further. Walter introduced the paper hats that

look like crowns, replicating a practice going back to the Roman
Saturnalia celebrations. Writers were commissioned to come up
with mottoes, puzzles, riddles and those awful corny jokes. Speciality
crackers of all shapes, sizes and designs were produced, and by the
end of the 19th century a peculiarly British Christmas tradition had
become well and truly established. Tom Smith Christmas Crackers
are still made today, and since 1909 exclusive Tom Smith crackers
have been manufactured for the British Royal Family.

The Queen's Speech

At 3 p.m. Greenwich Mean Time on Christmas Day, families in
Britain and many Commonwealth countries gather around the
television set or the radio, or, today, go on the internet, to listen to
the Queen's Christmas Message, an annual tradition that dates
back to 1932.

The first Royal Christmas Message was broadcast on BBC Radio
in 1932 by King George V at the suggestion of John Reith, first
Director General of the BBC, who was able to persuade the King
that the newly created Empire Service (now the World Service)
would enable him to speak in person to the whole of what was then
the British Empire. The king broadcast live from a small studio
at Sandringham and his speech, written by the author Rudyard
Kipling, was listened to by more than 20 million people across the
Empire, in Britain, Australia, Canada, South Africa and India.
During the Second World War, King George VI's broadcasts played
a huge role in boosting the morale of British troops overseas and
established the Christmas Message as an essential part of the British
Christmas Day. When Queen Elizabeth II made her first broadcast
in 1952 she sat in the same chair and at the same desk as her father
George VI and her grandfather George V had done. The first
televised Christmas message was broadcast from Sandringham in
1957 and for the first time millions of people could actually see the
Queen speaking to them in their own homes.

Today the Christmas Message is usually broadcast from
Buckingham Palace and recorded a few days before so that it can be
shown in countries such as New Zealand, Australia and Canada at
a time to suit them. Since 1997 the responsibility for producing and
broadcasting has been shared between the BBC and ITV and,
more recently, Sky Television.

The theme of the speech is chosen not by ministers or advisers
but by the monarch herself, and what gives the message its special
appeal is that is one of the rare times when the monarch is able to
share with all her people her own thoughts and reflections on the
concerns and issues of the day.

And so, exhausted but content, we move on to Boxing Day.

Boxing Day is celebrated on the day after Christmas, 26 December. In Britain, along with Australia, New Zealand, Canada and many Commonwealth countries, it is a public holiday, although in Britain, if Boxing Day falls on a Saturday or Sunday, the holiday is moved to the following Monday.

Why is it called Boxing Day? Well, churches in medieval Britain kept alms boxes at the back of the church in which people could place coins for the poor, and these boxes would be broken open on the day after Christmas to provide some relief for those who had nothing to eat after the communal feasting was over. Some collection boxes were shaped like a pig, hence the expression 'piggy bank'.

Servants were given the day off after Christmas, so they could rest or go and see their families after the hard work of cooking and waiting on their employers over the festivities. Sometimes they were given a box of leftovers, presents and coins to take home.

It was also customary for people to give a Christmas 'box' of gifts or money to tradesmen such as the butcher or the blacksmith, to thank them for their service over the year. In December 1663, Samuel Pepys writes in his diary of going to his shoemaker and giving 'something to the boys' box against Christmas'. This tradition has lasted to the present day as some people still like to leave a tip for their postman or dustmen.

It is thought that the Victorians first coined the term Boxing Day when they were busy reinventing Christmas in the 19th century.

Boxing Day is a secular invention and hosts many secular activities, in particular shopping. For many retailers, Boxing Day sales have taken over from the New Year sales as the most lucrative shopping day of the year.

Panto

Christmas pantomimes traditionally start on Boxing Day. 'Panto', as it is popularly called, has roots stretching right back to the Roman midwinter festival of Saturnalia where role-reversal was one of the key elements. In panto this is echoed in the tradition of the principal boy character being played by a girl and the comical pantomime dame being played by a man dressed in women's clothes. Panto also borrows audience participation and many of its stock characters from the medieval mummers' plays: notably the fool, or jester, and the wickedly evil 'baddie' – boo, hiss ... Likewise panto still keeps up the medieval tradition of having the baddie enter first from stage left, the evil 'hell' side, while the goodie follows from stage right, the 'heaven' side. Watch for it when you next go to see a pantomime.

Finally, music hall of the late 19th and early 20th century added the double entendres and backchat, the comic songs and the topical humour that make up the modern panto. Today's panto provides a painless and hugely enjoyable way to introduce children to live theatre, and the lead roles now attract stars of TV and film helping to bring in large and enthusiastic family audiences.

Sport

Boxing Day has long been a big day for sports of all kind, amateur and professional, with people enjoying the chance to go out and get some fresh air after the excesses of Christmas Day. As well as fun runs and charity events, many see a festive swim in the sea as an effective hangover cure.

Association Football

British football fans look forward to their club's Boxing Day fixture as one of the highlights of the season. The Boxing Day match has a long pedigree. The very first inter-club football match the world had ever seen was played on Boxing Day, in 1860, between the two oldest football clubs in the world, Sheffield FC and their close neighbours Hallam FC. The match was played at Hallam's Sandygate Road ground and Sheffield FC won 2–0.

Following the precedent set by that first club match, the inaugural football league season in 1888–89 included a Boxing Day fixture list, although right up until the 1950s football matches were played on Christmas Day as well. Sometimes clubs had to play two matches, one on Christmas Day and one on Boxing Day. The reason for this was that in those days footballers were working men who had to hold down a proper job and matches had to be arranged on their days off. The idea of playing sport on Christmas Day, however, became less popular in the 1950s as men increasingly wanted to be at home with their families and Christmas Day matches gradually disappeared from the football calendar, with the last such match being played in 1957. Today, because of the scarcity of public transport on Boxing Day, the football league tries to arrange local fixtures so that people don't have to travel too far to attend matches.

Cracker Joke
Who helped
Scrooge win
the Boxing Day
football game?

—

The ghost of
Christmas passed!

Horse Racing

Another sport that flourishes in Britain on Boxing Day is horse racing. Half a dozen or more race meetings are scheduled on Boxing Day every year, including the King George VI Chase at Kempton Park, which has been run on Boxing Day since 1947.

Boxing Day is also the biggest day of the year in the hunting calendar, with up to a quarter of a million people turning up to support some 250 Boxing Day hunt meets and events every year. Hunting with dogs was banned in 2004 and most hunts now go drag hunting, following an artificial scent.

Cricket

In Australia, since Boxing Day falls in the middle of the cricket season it is traditional to play a Test match on that day. The first Boxing Day Test match took place in Melbourne in 1950, with the fourth day's play of the Melbourne Test in that season's Ashes series between Australia and England. Then in 1974 the Third Test of the Ashes series started at Melbourne on Boxing Day and drew such huge crowds that it was decided to try and make a Boxing Day Test match a regular event. Since 1980 the Boxing Day Test has been played at the Melbourne Cricket Ground every year (except 1989) and the occasion has become a highlight of the cricket calendar and a cherished part of the Australian Christmas.

Cricket is also frequently played in New Zealand and South Africa on Boxing Day.

St Stephen's Day

Although Boxing Day is seen primarily as a secular celebration, there is a religious element to the day as well, with 26 December being the feast day of St Stephen. Indeed, in Ireland and many Catholic countries, it is known as St Stephen's Day rather than Boxing Day.

St Stephen is venerated as the first Christian martyr, having being stoned to death in AD 34 on the orders of the Jewish elders for preaching that Jesus was the Son of God. He was also the patron saint of horses, which may explain why horse racing is so popular on Boxing Day.

There is one particular carol that has become associated with Boxing Day and it is the one about Good King Wenceslas for, if you recall, he last looked out on the Feast of Stephen.

Wenceslas was a Duke of Bohemia, part of what is now the Czech Republic, early in the 10th century. He grew up in the Christian faith, recently introduced to Bohemia by his grandparents, and although he ruled for only a short time before he was assassinated by his jealous brother Boleslav, during that time he promoted Christianity, built numerous churches, introduced a good education system and established an effective law and order framework. Stories grew up of his good works and generosity to the poor and Wenceslas became recognised as a martyr and a saint, becoming the first Czech saint and the patron saint of the Czech state. He is buried in St Vitus Cathedral on the site of the St Vitus Church which he founded within Prague Castle in 930. The central square in Prague is named Wenceslas Square in his honour, and his statue in the square is a rallying point for the affirmation of Czech nationalism.

Good King Wenceslas looked out
On the feast of Stephen
When the snow lay round about
Deep and crisp and even.

The carol by which the good king Wenceslas has been immortalised was written in 1853 by an Anglican priest called John Mason Neale, Warden of East Sackville College in East Grinstead in Sussex. Neal took the story from a poem composed by Czech poet Václav Svoboda just a few years earlier in 1847, and the music from a 13th-century carol called 'Tempus Adest Floridum', 'The Time for Flowering', from *Piae Cantiones*, a collection of songs from Finland published in 1582.

Cracker Joke
How does Good King Wenceslas like his pizzas?

—

Deep pan, crisp and even!

Although there is no mention of the Nativity in the song, 'Good King Wenceslas' has become one of our most popular, if least understood, Christmas carols.

And so, with Boxing Day, we have come to the end of our investigation into Christmas. Although of course, if you've been concentrating, you will know that we are only into Day Two of the Twelve Days of Christmas. There are still another ten days to go to Twelfth Night when we can take down the decorations.

Nevertheless we have examined the pagan roots of Christmas, how it was carried to most of the known world through the Roman Empire, shaped through the Middle Ages, particularly in Germany, banned by the Puritans and finally reinvented in England, largely by Prince Albert and Charles Dickens, and in America, largely by Washington Irving, Clement Clarke Moore and Thomas Nast.

And are we any the wiser? Probably not. But hasn't it been fun?

'At Christmas play and make good cheer,
for Christmas comes but once a year.'

Thomas Tusser, 16th-century farmer and poet

A Fun Recap

The Book of Christmas

1)   Jesus' birthday is not mentioned in the Bible. December 25th was chosen because it was the shortest day of the year and coincided with the pagan winter solstice festivals that the Church authorities wanted Christmas to supplant. In fact, Jesus' birthday could not have been in December because the shepherds to whom the angels brought the news of his birth 'abiding in the field, keeping watch over their flock by night…' In December, sheep would not be out in the field.

2)   The Druids decorated evergreen trees during their winter celebrations, hanging nuts and fruits from the branches as gifts for the winter deities.

3)   The modern Christmas tree evolved out of the Paradise tree, which was hung with apples and used in medieval Paradise plays to represent the Tree of Knowledge from the Garden of Paradise.

4)   Mistletoe is the Saxon word for 'dung twig', so called because it is spread through bird droppings. The Druids thought mistletoe possessed magic qualities since it remained green during the winter – so when harvesting mistletoe, which grows on trees and not in the ground, it must not be allowed to fall to the ground or it loses its magic.

5)   The first ever Christmas card was sent in 1843 by Sir Henry Cole, the man who designed the world's first postage stamp, the Penny Black. It showed that longstanding Christmas tradition, a family drinking wine, and caused some controversy as a child was shown apparently being offered some wine.

6)   Because of their red uniforms Victorian postmen were nick-named 'robins' and this is why robins began to appear on Christmas cards.

7)   Two of the three bestselling Christmas songs of all time, Irving Berlin's White Christmas, and Mel Torme's The Christmas Song (Chestnuts Roasting on an Open Fire) were both written in the California sunshine; White Christmas in 1940 by a swimming pool in Beverley Hills and The Christmas Song in 1945 during a hot summer in the San Fernando Valley.

8)   The Christmas song that earns the highest amount of royalties every year (£500,000) is Slade's Merry Christmas Everybody, which was first released in 1973.

9)   Santa Claus's tunic was not always red, it was often green or blue. It was the American cartoonist Thomas Nast who gave Santa his red coat in his cartoons for Harper's Weekly in the 1860s and 1870s, based on St Nicolas' red bishop's robes. Fortunately for Coca Cola, their corporate colour was the same colour as Santa's red tunic and so they used Santa Claus in their adverts, leading many people to think that Coca Cola was responsible for Santa's tunic being red.

10)   Henry VIII was the first person to eat turkey for Christmas. But turkey was expensive so, until the 20th century, the traditional Christmas bird was a goose.

11)   Christmas pudding was originally a soup or stew boiled in a cauldron over a wood fire.

12)   The last Sunday before Advent is known as 'Stir-up Sunday' when every family member is supposed to take a turn to stir the Christmas pudding mix while making a wish.

13)   One Brussels sprout contains more vitamin C than an orange.

14)   It is said that if you eat a mince pie on every one of the twelve days of Christmas you will have good health for the next year.

15)   The Christmas cracker was invented in 1840 by a London confectioner called Tom Smith, who was inspired by a French sweet wrapped in a twist of paper called a bob-bon.

16)   The first Christmas Message was given by King George V on BBC Radio in 1932. It was written by Rudyard Kipling.

17)   Boxing Day is so called because it is the day on which money was distributed from the church poor boxes.

158

About the Author

Christopher Winn is a freelance writer and historian, and has been a collector of trivia for over 20 years. He has worked with Terry Wogan and Jonathan Ross and on BBC's Children in Need. He has written for the *Spectator, Daily Mail, Daily Telegraph, Guardian, Daily Express* and *The Field* and sets quiz questions for television and national newspapers. Winn's first bestselling *I Never Knew That* series has sold over one million copies.

Acknowledgements

All my thanks to Kajal Mistry and to her team at Hardie Grant.
Without their guidance and enthusiasm this book would never
have happened.

A special thanks to Eila Purvis for her patience and forbearance
and for all her hard work in spotting my mistakes and knocking
the manuscript into shape.

Thanks especially the designers at NotOnSundy and to Hollie
Brown for the wonderful illustrations.

Bibliography

A Visit from St Nicholas: Clement Clarke Moore
(pub anonymously 1823)

Arthur Christopher Benson: The Life of Edward White Benson:
Sometime Archbishop of Canterbury

Catholic Encyclopedia

Charles Dickens: A Christmas Carol

Clement A Miles: Christmas in Ritual and Tradition,
Christian and Pagan T F Unwin 1913

Encyclopedia Britannica

John Stow: The Survey of London pub 1603

Old Farmer's Almanac www.almanac.com

stnicholascenter.org

Victoria and Albert Museum vam.ac.uk

Washington Irving: A History of New-York